JESUS

PAUL JOHNSON

VIKING

Jesus

A Biography from a Believer.

VIKING
Published by the Penguin Group
Penguin Group (USA) Inc., 375 Hudson Street, New York, New York 10014, U.S.A.
Penguin Group (Canada), 90 Eglinton Avenue East, Suite 700, Toronto, Ontario,
Canada M4P 2Y3 (a division of Pearson Penguin Canada Inc.)
Penguin Books Ltd, 80 Strand, London WC2R 0RL, England
Penguin Ireland, 25 St. Stephen's Green, Dublin 2, Ireland (a division of Penguin Books Ltd)
Penguin Books Australia Ltd, 250 Camberwell Road, Camberwell, Victoria 3124,
Australia (a division of Pearson Australia Group Pty Ltd)
Penguin Books India Pvt Ltd, 11 Community Centre, Panchsheel Park, New Delhi–110 017, India
Penguin Group (NZ), 67 Apollo Drive, Rosedale, North Shore 0632, New Zealand
(a division of Pearson New Zealand Ltd)
Penguin Books (South Africa) (Pty) Ltd, 24 Sturdee Avenue, Rosebank, Johannesburg 2196, South Africa

Penguin Books Ltd, Registered Offices: 80 Strand, London WC2R 0RL, England

First published in 2010 by Viking Penguin, a member of Penguin Group (USA) Inc.

10 9 8 7 6 5 4 3 2 1

LIBRARY OF CONGRESS CATALOGING-IN-PUBLICATION DATA
Johnson, Paul, 1928–
Jesus : a biography from a believer / Paul Johnson.
p. cm.
Includes bibliographical references and index.
ISBN 978-0-670-02159-8
1. Jesus Christ—Biography. I. Title.
BT301.3.J64 2010
232.9'01—dc22
[B]   2009047214

Printed in the United States of America · Set in Goudy Old Style · Designed by Amy Hill

To my mother,
Anne Johnson,
who first taught me about Jesus

Contents

INTRODUCTION: Man and God *1*

I Birth, Childhood, Youth *9*

II Baptism, Temptation, and the Apostles *35*

III The Danger of the Miracles *57*

IV What Jesus Taught and Why *79*

V Poetry and Parables, Questions and Silence *97*

VI Encounters: Men, Women, Children, the Aged *125*

VII Jesus's New Ten Commandments *155*

VIII Jesus's Trial and Crucifixion *177*

IX The Resurrection and the Birth of Christianity *209*

Further Reading *229*

Index *231*

JESUS

✝ Man and God

J ESUS OF NAZARETH WAS, in terms of his influence, the most important human being in history. He is also the most written about and discussed. The earliest surviving document dealing with him, St. Paul's First Epistle to the Corinthians, was circulated (that is, copied and published) in the fifties of the first century AD, about twenty years after his death. By then, biographies of him written in the Aramaic tongue he normally spoke were circulating, but these have since disappeared. Within half a century of his death, however, four biographies, written in Greek, had been published, and all have come down to us. By the end of the century, forty-five authentic documents about him had appeared, and these have also survived. Since then, first documents, then entire books about him have been published in growing quantity, and in all languages. Today, there are over one hundred thousand printed biographies of Jesus in English alone, and many more monographs. More than one hundred were issued in the first decade of the twenty-first century.

The religion which commemorates Jesus's teachings, death, and Resurrection was well established in half a dozen countries by AD 50. His followers were already known as "Christians," a term joyfully adopted by the faithful, even though it was coined in Antioch, a city notorious for its slang neologisms. The number of Christians has increased ever since, and is now about 1.25 billion. Although static or declining in some parts of the world, Christianity is growing in Asia and Latin America, and especially in Africa. The first Christian place of worship dates from about AD 50, and the now nearly one million chapels, churches, basilicas, abbeys, and cathedrals include many of the largest, most remarkable, and beautiful buildings ever erected: indeed, the influence of Christianity has been perhaps the single biggest factor in the development of architecture over the last two millennia. The image of Jesus is the most favored subject matter in painting and sculpture, and the Christian influence is similarly predominant in poetry, music, and all the other arts, except photography, the cinema, and the electronic media, though even in these Christ's likeness is common. In many ways—and in cultural and moral respects especially—Jesus's life, and the faith it created, are the central events in the history of humanity, around which all revolves not only today but, I foresee, in the future.

So far we have considered the influence of Jesus as man. But the reason he has been so important as a man is not merely his human nature and personality, or his actions, but the fact, which all Christians have believed as I believe, that he was and is God, too. The unique event of someone both God and man appearing on earth is the essence of Christianity. What is the explanation for this singular phenomenon? It is a mystery, as are so many of the fundamental questions which face us in life, and we can only conjecture. How to make humans worthy of existing alongside their Creator? The answer is provided in John 3:16: "For God so loved the world, that he gave his only begotten Son, that whosoever believeth in him should not perish, but have everlasting life."

Since God is omniscient and omnipresent, we must assume that this scheme of salvation, and this ultimate human conse-quence, was prefigured in the creation of time and space, and that therefore God was, ab initio, Trinitarian in nature, mono-theistic but also three in one: Father, Son, and Holy Spirit. Why was the salvation process made operative in 4 BC with the birth of Jesus and not sooner or later? Since God exists outside space and time, which are mere ephemeral devices to enable humanity to evolve and be tested, then saved, the ques-tion (natural though it seems to me) is nugatory. It is also futile for us to inquire into the nature of Jesus and God, and his preexistence from the beginning, since that is unknowable, let alone the future, which is still hidden from us.

What we can do, however, is write about Jesus the man, during his life in which, in the words of St. John, he "dwelt among us . . . full of grace and truth" (1:14). His life has been written more often than that of any other human being, with infinite variations of detail, employing vast resources of scholarship, and often controversially, not to say acrimoniously. Scholarship, like everything else, is subject to fashion, and it was the fashion, in the late nineteenth and early twentieth centuries, for some to deny that Jesus existed. No serious scholar holds that view now, and it is hard to see how it ever took hold, for the evidence of Jesus's existence is abundant. Roman secular writers much closer to his time, such as Pliny, Tacitus, and Suetonius, took it for granted, as did the accurate and conscientious Jewish historian Josephus, writing in the generation after Jesus's death. Moreover, unlike the overwhelming majority of famous figures in antiquity, whose existence has never been questioned, Jesus was the subject of four biographies, one written by an eyewitness, the others transcripts of verbal accounts by eyewitnesses, all made public within thirty to forty years of his death, and all agreeing in essentials. They are confirmed in many details by contemporary letters circulated by Jesus's followers.

The problem with writing the life of Jesus the man is not so much the paucity of sources as their abundance, and the difficulty in reaching behind the written text to the full meaning of sayings and episodes which need to be explained afresh to each generation. There is the further problem of presenting to readers, two millennia later, the personality of a man so extraordinary and protean, passionate yet deliberative, straightforward and subtle, full of authority and even, at times, stern, yet also infinitely kind, understanding, forgiving, and loving, so dazzling in his excellences that those close to him had no hesitation in accepting his divinity. Yet it is one of the glories of Christianity that writers of all periods have felt it possible to venture their own portraits of the man.

The sketch that follows, broad of brush and yet pointillist on occasion, reflects many years of reading and historical study. Apart from references to the Gospel texts (all in the King James Version), I do not cite my authorities, though I am prepared to defend all my assertions, if challenged, by documentation. My objects have been clarity and brevity, and my desire is to convey the joy and nourishment I receive in following Jesus's footsteps and pondering his words.

I

✝ Birth, Childhood, Youth

THE WORLD INTO WHICH Jesus was born was harsh, cruel, violent, and unstable. It was also materialistic and increasingly wealthy. The great fact of geopolitics was Rome and its possessions, in the process of transforming itself from a republic into an empire. It now occupied the shores of the entire Mediterranean, from which one of its great men, Pompey, had driven all the pirates which once infested it, using ruthless methods of brutality, torture, and large-scale public executions. As a result, trade was expanding fast and many cities and individuals doubled their riches in the generation before Jesus was born.

Rome, pushing inland from the Mediterranean, now occupied all of Italy and Spain, as well as Greece and Egypt, and what we call Turkey. Between 50 and 60 million people now came under its laws. Fifty years before Jesus was born, Julius Caesar had added the whole of Gaul (modern France) to Roman territory, and he had even carried out two reconnaissances to Britain, though it was not conquered until fifteen years after Jesus's death. The expanding empire was based upon muscle power rather than technology, thanks to about 15 million slaves, who constituted one-third of the population in the towns, and whose life was summed up by Aristotle in four words: "work, punishment, and food." The cost of two years' food bought a skilled slave. Though neither scientists nor technicians, the Romans were lawyers and builders. Their laws were uniform throughout the civilized world and enforced with horrific severity, the instrument of justice being the crucifix on which malefactors were nailed and left to die. The Romans made superb roads, and they had discovered the virtues of cement, which, when mixed with agglomerates, constituted concrete. The Roman Empire was built on concrete: it enabled the Romans to create immense aqueducts to bring fresh water to their cities, as well as to erect huge public buildings. Rome had not produced a culture as splendid as that of Greece. Most of the statues which adorned its cities were copies of Greek models, and it had nothing so fine as the Athens Parthenon to show. But the Forum in Rome was already spectacular in its grandeur, and the city's Pantheon, being built in Jesus's lifetime, was revolutionary in its enclosure of vast space. Rome had a growing literature, too. Its national poet, Virgil, died fifteen years before Jesus was born, and its greatest lyricist, Horace, four years before. But Ovid, its love poet, was still alive, aged thirty-nine in 4 BC. Livy completed his great history of Rome when Jesus was a teenager. Seneca, a dramatist and philosopher, was born in the same year as Jesus. The great marble sculpture known as *Laocoön and His Sons,* now in the Vatican Museums, was created in his childhood.

The cultural efflorescence of Jesus's day was made possible by the stability imposed by Caesar's heir, Octavian, who became Rome's first emperor as Augustus Caesar, following the civil war. He died when Jesus was eighteen, but under his successor, Tiberius, Rome was so terrified of his Praetorian Guard that the emperor was able to live on the island of Capri, amid its pleasures, while his guard's commander, Sejanus, kept all in peace. In what we now call Palestine, a similar calm prevailed at the time of Jesus's birth, under the plutocratic tyranny of Herod the Great. For more than thirty years, this astute financier, who had made himself the richest individual in the entire empire, had by his subservience to the rulers of Rome (and by princely gifts) made himself master of the ancient kingdom of the Jews. He was the greatest builder of his age, creating a new port at Caesarea in Samaria, rebuilding and enlarging the Temple in Jerusalem, and building public baths, aqueducts, and what we would call shopping centers in half a dozen cities, as well as a ring of powerful fortresses, including the massive Antonia (named after Mark Antony) in Jerusalem, overlooking the Temple and his own enormous palace. He was a benefactor of the Jews on a colossal scale. But he was not popular among them. Only half Jewish by birth, and wholly Greek in his cultural tastes, he was regarded as heretical by the Jewish religious authorities for sponsoring Greek-style games, theaters, and music. He also had numerous wives and concubines, some of them Gentiles, and sired many children. Suspicious and cruel, he slaughtered over forty of his wives, children, and close relatives, often in circumstances of peculiar atrocity, for conspiracies, real or imaginary, against his rule and person. As his reign drew to a close—the last year of his life was the year of Jesus's birth—his suspicions increased, and an atmosphere of paranoia prevailed at his court.

Yet Herod's kingdom was prosperous, and Galilee, though regarded as wild and primitive by the sophisticated urban Jews of Jerusalem, was not backward economically. Galilean Jews ate well. There was an abundance of sheep, bred for wool as well as meat. The ubiquitous presence of sheep and shepherds is the background of Jesus's life and the source of his most frequent images. Grain, grown in abundance, was cheap and exported through Caesarea. Bread, "the staff of life," was eaten at all meals, and it, too, was a source of constant imagery for Jesus. Olive trees were plentiful, and a variety of olives, black, green, and white, was part of the daily fare and made into oil for cooking. There was a wide range of vegetables, salads, and spices. Wine was drunk at the principal meals.

Jews helped one another, and their communities ran privately organized welfare schemes for the sick, the infirm, and orphans. Needy widows were assisted. There were poor Jews, who received doles from their brethren, but most of those referred to in the Gospels as "the poor" or "beggars" were non-Jews, for all parts of Palestine were mixed-race societies, with immigrants, detribalized peasants, and nomads forming a large part of the population. Giving to "the poor" was part of the duty of every self-respecting Jew, and it, too, was part of the imagery of Jesus's life.

Nazareth was a small Galilean town in 4 BC, home to many small workshops and craftsmen. One was Joseph, a carpenter, who believed himself descended from King David and could recite his pedigree. He was probably literate (in Aramaic, the vernacular, and sacred Hebrew), as were the majority of Jews. He had taken as his future bride a teenager, aged sixteen or so, called Mary, also from the house of David and very likely related to him. She lived behind or above his workshop but was still a virgin. Their marriage was to take place in the following year. She came from a respectable home, could read and write, cook, weave, and sew, and was preparing to be a diligent wife to a prosperous tradesman. She had a capacious memory, and many years later was to be a principal source for St. Luke, the Greek-speaking doctor whose Gospel deals most fully with Jesus's birth and childhood.

All well-nurtured Jews read the scriptures, especially the Torah, which were the nation's record of its history, its spiritual guide, and its book of prayer. Mary was thus occupied when the angel Gabriel appeared and, according to Luke (1:28–38), said to her: "Hail, thou that art highly favoured, the Lord is with thee: blessed art thou among women." This astonishing greeting troubled and puzzled her. But Gabriel said, "Fear not, Mary: for thou hast found favour with God. And, behold, thou shalt conceive in thy womb, and bring forth a son, and shalt call his name JESUS." The angel went on: "He shall be great, and shall be called the Son of the Highest: and the Lord God shall give unto him the throne of his father David: And he shall reign over the house of Jacob for ever; and of his kingdom there shall be no end."

We can be sure that Mary remembered these words exactly. She also recalled her first, anxious question—"How shall this be, since I am still a virgin?" (or, as she put it, "seeing I know not a man?")—and the angel's explicit reply: "The Holy Ghost shall come upon thee, and the power of the Highest shall overshadow thee: therefore also that holy thing which shall be born of thee shall be called the Son of God."

To these dramatic words the angel added a personal note.

Her cousin Elizabeth, he informed Mary, had also, in her old age, conceived a son, and was now six months pregnant. It was this startling piece of family news which finally brought home to Mary the reality of the angel's message. She now submitted to her destiny in memorable words reflecting a proud humility: "Behold the handmaid of the Lord; be it unto me according to thy word."

There is no more touching scene in the whole of history than Gabriel's disclosure to the trembling Virgin that she is pregnant, and her brave acceptance of the fact as an honor: no wonder so many of the greatest Western artists have endeavored to bring the episode to life as "the Annunciation." For a teenager, Mary was notably energetic and decisive. She wanted the news of her cousin Elizabeth's condition confirmed, and she immediately set forth, alone, on a long journey into the hill country of Judah, where Elizabeth lived with her husband, Zacharias, a priest who was a part-time official of the Jerusalem Temple.

The second notable scene in the story of Jesus occurred when Mary arrived there, recorded by Luke. Upon seeing Mary, Elizabeth felt her child, the future St. John the Baptist, leap in her womb, and the Holy Spirit intimated to her, at once, that Mary, too, was pregnant and carried God's son within her. "[W]ith a loud voice" Elizabeth said, "Blessed art thou among women, and blessed is the fruit of thy womb. And whence is this to me, that the mother of my Lord should come to me?" (Lk 1:41–43).

Mary's reply to this salutation is one of the most striking passages in the New Testament. She replied in words which fall easily into verse, the form in which I have taken the liberty of transcribing them, and they have often been set to music (Lk 1:46–55):

My soul doth magnify the Lord,

And my spirit hath rejoiced in God my Saviour.

For he hath regarded the low estate of his
handmaiden:

for, behold, from henceforth all generations shall call
me blessed.

For he that is mighty hath done to me great things;
and holy is his name.

And his mercy is on them that fear him from
generation to generation.

He hath shewed strength with his arm; he hath scattered
the proud in the imagination of their hearts.

He hath put down the mighty from their seats, and
exalted them of low degree.

He hath filled the hungry with good things; and the
rich he hath sent empty away.

This great hymn of exaltation, rightly known as the Magnificat, lifts the spirits of the poor and humble, and adumbrates one of the central themes of Jesus's ministry. Within the Gospel story there is not only truth but its fruit, beauty, and here was Mary, while still carrying Jesus in her womb, creating poetry of mighty power.

Luke says Mary stayed three months with Elizabeth. She then returned to Nazareth and told Joseph of her condition. According to the Gospel of St. Matthew (1:19–25), which in many respects is the most detailed and is based upon Aramaic sources, her fiancé, who had treated her as a virgin, was shocked by her news. "[B]eing a just man," however, he was "not willing to make her a publick example, [but] was minded to put her away privily. . . . [W]hile he thought on these things," an angel appeared to him "in a dream" and said, "[F]ear not to take unto thee Mary thy wife: for that which is conceived in her is of the Holy Ghost. And she shall bring forth a son, and thou shalt call his name JESUS: for he shall save his people from their sins." Matthew says that Joseph did as the angel bid "and took unto him his wife." Matthew says that Joseph did not cohabit with Mary until Jesus was born. Indeed, the most ancient traditions insist that Mary remained a virgin all her life, though Joseph gave her and her child all the love and care of a devoted husband.

The next episode occurred four or five months later, when

a decree of the emperor, Augustus, for a census needed for taxation was passed on to all Herod's subjects by Cyrenius, the governor of Syria. They were commanded to register at their native towns. As both Joseph and Mary were of David's house, they went (Mary "great with child," as noted in Luke 2:5) to Jerusalem, the city David had added to the Jewish kingdom by conquest, and in particular to Bethlehem, a small, one-street town six miles away, which was particularly associated with David's name. Mary was a sturdy teenager. This was her third long journey while pregnant. Once in Bethlehem, "the days were accomplished that she should be delivered. And she brought forth her firstborn son, and wrapped him in swaddling clothes, and laid him in a manger; because there was no room for them in the inn" (Lk 2:6–7). About a century later, Justin Martyr, who came from about forty miles away and repeated local tradition, said the manger was a cave; that is not unlikely, for there are many in the limestone ridge on which Bethlehem perches.

There is no mention of a doctor or midwife, and Joseph seems to have been Mary's only attendant. But she had no need of help. She ministered to herself, and her baby was, and remained throughout his life, healthy. But there were visitors (Lk 2:8–18; Mt 2:1–12). According to Luke, local shepherds, "keeping watch over their flock by night," were startled by an astonishing light, which they recognized as an angelic vision—

"and they were sore afraid." But they were told by the angel: "Fear not: for, behold, I bring you good tidings of great joy. . . . For unto you is born this day in the city of David a Saviour, which is Christ the Lord. . . . Ye shall find the babe wrapped in swaddling clothes, lying in a manger." Suddenly there was a heavenly chorus singing, "Glory to God in the highest, and on earth peace, good will toward men." The shepherds decided to go to Bethlehem, and they found Jesus, Mary, and Joseph, just as the angel said, in a stable. They explained all this to local people, and "all they that heard it wondered." They also told Mary of the light, and the angel, and the chorus, so that she "kept all these things, and pondered them in her heart."

What Luke did not describe, but Matthew did, were the next visitors, "wise men from the east." They brought gifts: gold, frankincense, and myrrh, "treasures" as Matthew called them, fit for a king. For the wise men were astrologers, used to studying the heavens and prognosticating from the changing configurations of the stars. One star in particular they believed denoted by its position that a king had been born to the Jews. They came to Jerusalem and presented themselves at Herod's court, asking to be given directions. Herod "gathered all the chief priests and the scribes of the people together" and asked them to indicate from the scriptures where the king, or savior, or Christ, as prophesied, would be born. They replied: Bethlehem. Herod saw the wise men "privily" and sent them to Bethlehem:

"Go and search diligently for the young child; and when ye have found him, bring me word again, that I may come and worship him also."

The wise men, and their story of the newborn baby who was to be king of the Jews, aroused all Herod's paranoia. Matthew says that "being warned of God in a dream that they should not return to Herod, they departed into their own country another way." Joseph, too, was warned in a dream that he, Mary, and the child were endangered by Herod. He was told, "Arise, and take the young child and his mother, and flee into Egypt, and be thou there until I bring thee word: for Herod will seek the young child to destroy him." Joseph did as he was told. The "flight into Egypt" has become another of those memorable episodes which has inspired artists over the ages—it is the subject of Caravaggio's finest work, now in the Doria Pamphilj Gallery in Rome. The little party is seen resting. Joseph holds up a musical score for a young angel to play a lullaby, while Mary and the baby sleep.

Herod's terror that the infant king would steal his kingdom led to his greatest crime in his long life of misdeeds. He dispatched armed assassins "and slew all the children that were in Bethlehem, and in all the coasts thereof, from two years old and under" (Mt 2:16). It was his last act. Within weeks he was dead. His territories were divided, and his son Archelaus inherited Judaea. Joseph was told this, and returned with his family. But he was careful to avoid Judaea, for fear Archelaus would have inherited his father's suspicious nature, and returned to Nazareth in Galilee by a roundabout route, through Gaza and Samaria.

The story of the birth of Jesus, and the visits of the shepherds and the wise men, is the idyllic side of the Nativity, giving Jesus's infancy a delightful storybook quality which has entranced everyone, young and old, for two thousand years. But the massacre of the innocents, as it came to be known, reminds us of the darker side of life in an obscure province of the Roman Empire in the first century AD: the atrocious, unbridled cruelty of power, the absence in practice of any rule of law to restrain the powerful, and the contempt for human life, even the tenderest, shown by the mighty. This was the reality of human wickedness which Jesus was born to redress, against which he spoke, and which finally engulfed him. The massacre of the innocents is a foretaste of Calvary.

Some few people could see into this future, as is recorded in Luke (1:13–23, 59–65). He writes that Elizabeth's husband, Zacharias, was skeptical when the angel Gabriel told him that his elderly wife was pregnant with the future John the Baptist, and as punishment was struck dumb. But when the child was born and taken to be circumcised, Elizabeth refused to name him after his father and insisted he be called John. Her neighbors and cousins protested: "There is none of thy kindred that is called by this name. And they made signs to his father, how he would have him called." To their astonishment, Zacharias "asked for a writing table, and wrote: saying, His name is John. And they marvelled all." More remarkable still, "his mouth was opened immediately, and his tongue loosed, and he spake, and praised God." But, as with so many incidents in the story of Jesus, this happy tale is overshadowed by the threatening world surrounding it. News of the remarkable birth must have spread and reached Herod's ever-suspicious ears. An ancient tradition, published by the early fathers, such as Origen, says Herod had Zacharias slaughtered "between the temple and the altar." So he is venerated as an early martyr.

There was another old priest who did duty at the Temple called Simeon. Luke says he was "just and devout," firmly believing in the coming Messiah. Indeed, he had had a revelation "that he should not see death, before he had seen the Lord's Christ" (2:25–26). When Mary and Joseph came to the Temple for Mary's ritual purification after giving birth and for Jesus's circumcision—both according to Judaic law—the old man was present and took the child into his arms, blessed God in thanks, and said, using poetic words which have echoed down the generations (2:29–32):

> Lord, now lettest thou thy servant depart in peace,
> according to thy word:

> For mine eyes have seen thy salvation,
>
> Which thou hast prepared before the face of all people;
>
> A light to lighten the Gentiles, and the glory of thy
>
> people Israel.

But, continues Luke (2:34–40), turning to Mary, the old man also said, on the somber note which alternates with the joyous tone of those early episodes in Jesus's life, "Behold, this child is set for the fall and rising again of many in Israel; ... ([and] a sword shall pierce through thy own soul also,) that the thoughts of many hearts may be revealed." He was joined by an old woman called Anna, described by Luke as a "prophetess" and "a widow of about fourscore and four years," who "served God with fastings and prayers night and day." She, too, recognized the child as the Redeemer. The forecasts and warnings of Anna and Simeon joined the other words which Mary treasured in her heart. She did not fail to note that, expanding the prophecies, her child would be "a light of the Gentiles"—indeed the entire human race—and not just Jews, and that his sacrifices would pierce her like a sword. As "the child grew, and waxed strong in spirit, filled with wisdom," she must have spent many anxious hours pondering his destiny and the atrocious pain, as well as joy, it would bring her.

She told Luke of one striking episode (2:42–51) which confirmed her hopes for him but puzzled her understanding. She,

Joseph, and the child formed a close trio, well termed "the Holy Family" in Christian devotion. There was great piety in their home at Nazareth, much praying, and the Jewish feasts and practices were meticulously observed. Every year at the feast of Passover, they went up to Jerusalem to make a sacrifice in the Temple. This testifies to Joseph's success in his trade, and the comparative affluence in which they lived, for the long and expensive journey meant that Joseph was away from his work for many weeks. In this annual pilgrimage they had many "kinsfolk and acquaintance." When Jesus was twelve, they thought him old enough to wander about by himself, exploring. The Temple, rebuilt by Herod on a gigantic scale, was a vast labyrinth of courts, rooms, and corridors, and Jerusalem itself a major city of palaces and forts, and a warren of houses. When the time came to leave, "Jesus tarried behind in Jerusalem; and Joseph and his mother knew not of it." They assumed he was with their friends in the convoy of mules and donkeys and had gone "a day's journey" before, suddenly frightened, they realized he had been left behind in the holy and wicked city.

Luke records that after three days of frantic searching "they found him in the temple, sitting in the midst of the doctors, both hearing them, and asking them questions. And all that heard him were astonished at his understanding and answers." Here speaks an adoring mother's pride, no doubt, but the next exchange she remembers is rather different and unexpected. She rebuked Jesus for his thoughtlessness: "Son, why hast thou thus dealt with us? behold, thy father and I have sought thee sorrowing." He replied, "[W]ist ye not that I must be about my Father's business?" Luke adds: "[T]hey understood not the saying which he spake unto them." It is striking that these first recorded words of Jesus are of a piece with his entire life and mission: he must be about God's business. And though Mary, by courtesy, refers to Joseph as his father, Jesus already knows and believes his Father is God, and says so, without any attempt at concealment.

Mary, Luke adds, "kept all these sayings in her heart." But it is at this point that the stories she related of Jesus's conception, birth, and childhood cease abruptly. Jesus went back to Nazareth with Mary and Joseph, "and was subject unto them." Luke then skips the next eighteen years of Jesus's life and moves to his baptism by St. John. The other evangelists are likewise silent. It is a somber and unwelcome fact that for more than half of Jesus's life we know absolutely nothing about what he did or where he went or how he lived.

We can be sure he was well instructed. Virtually all clever Jewish children were, if circumstances permitted, and Jesus came from a comfortable home. We know he could read, for his deep and, still more, his skeptical knowledge of the scriptures is evidence of constant study of the texts from an early age. By age twelve he was perfectly capable of taking part in a learned discussion of their meaning. We know he could write, too, though there is only one recorded instance of his doing so. This was the occasion when he stopped the puritanical but hypocritical Jews from stoning to death a woman taken in adultery by writing their own sins in the dust. The fact that he performed this difficult feat, and that his writing was instantly read and understood, argues that he had an unusually clear and readable hand, almost the hand of a professional scribe, one might think. But no writing by Jesus has survived. Nor do we know what he read, apart from the scriptures.

What we do know, from the records of his sayings, is that he was a civilized, cultured, educated man who chose his words with great care and precision, with delicacy, accuracy, and tact—all indications of wide reading in secular as well as religious literature. My belief is that he was familiar with Latin and Greek, as well as his native Aramaic and the Hebrew he spoke and read as an educated observant Jew. His habitual poetic turn of phrase, though natural to him (as to his mother), was also, I suspect, acquired by steady reading of poetry, much of which he had learned by heart. This poetry, I think, included not just Hebrew texts like the book of Job, which is full of poetry, and the religious songs we call the Psalms, but the treasury of Greek poets that circulated in the empire by this time. I believe Jesus could have recited passages from Homer and Euripides, possibly Virgil also. But this is mere deductive supposition.

We must assume that Jesus was self-taught in many respects. His words and concepts betray absolutely no sign of academic deformation or the impress of a system. He repudiated such things, just as he hated legalism in moral teaching. His was an imagination unsullied by the classroom or lecture hall. Being an autodidact, he had never attended such places, and so was dismissed by his critics as uneducated. John reports that the Temple Jews, amazed at his teaching there, sneered, "How knoweth this man letters, having never learned?" (7:15). We can only guess where the young Jesus found his books to study. But written materials of all kinds were never rare in the Jewish world, even in a country town like Nazareth.

What is less conjectural is that Jesus was a man of wide knowledge, especially of trade and agriculture. This is made clear by his confident and expert references to those practical matters in his sayings and parables. Jesus had a huge range, one reason why so many loved to listen to him, often picking up approvingly a reference to their own calling. But I suspect his knowledge reflected actual experience. The death of Joseph, which occurred during his missing years, led to the breakup of the Nazareth household; Mary went to live with one or another of her numerous family or clan, which included a sister and grown-up children, sometimes referred to as Jesus's brothers, or brethren.

At this point it would have been natural for Jesus, who had evidently chosen not to carry on Joseph's workshop as a carpenter, to leave home and seek experience in a wider world, so as to carry on, in due course, his "Father's business" more efficiently. There is no means of knowing what he did. One suggestion is that he became an Essene. But his teaching and behavior are so foreign to what we know of this sect from the Dead Sea Scrolls that it can be ruled out. Nor is it likely he belonged to any other religious sect, of which there were many. Zealotry of any kind was foreign to him. He bore none of the psychological stigmata of the professional cleric, monk, or anchorite, being moderate, disliking religiosity and strict observance, moving easily and enjoyably with men and women of all degrees and temperaments, and shunning solitude, except for prayer. He was a convivial and collegiate spirit, always seeking companions and new friends.

All this argues wide experience of different callings. I think Jesus may have deliberately moved from one job to another, to acquire knowledge not just of work but of diverse men and women. That is one reason he delayed beginning his mission until he was thirty. He must certainly have been involved in agriculture, about which he knew much. I believe he was for some time a shepherd. Sheep and their care are so pervasive in his sayings, and the nature of the Good Shepherd so central to his teaching, that I think this calling had a special place not only in his experience but in his affection. Those rough men who crowded round his crib at birth made him, as it were, an honorary shepherd for life. His experience as a shepherd would also help to explain his love of high places for important moments in his life, and his habit of punctuating his normal conviviality with periods of solitude for prayer.

This, then, is what we know of Jesus's birth and childhood, and what we can reasonably guess about his life from twelve to thirty. At that point he began his ministry and entered the full glare of evangelical record.

II

✝ Baptism, Temptation, and the Apostles

THE LAND IN WHICH Jesus began his ministry was prosperous but unsettled and far from tranquil, seething with rumors of miraculous events to come, liable to sudden gatherings of popular masses, tinder-dry and explosive, difficult to govern. Both its Roman rulers and the puppet kings and high priests to whom they delegated some power put keeping the peace above any other public object. They were particularly wary of spiritual rabble-rousers in the Jewish tradition of prophets. There were probably over three million Jews, over a million in Galilee alone, and about 10 percent of the inhabitants of the Roman Empire were affected by Jewish teaching in some way. Judaic monotheism, with its doctrinal certainties and detailed moral teaching, was popular among serious, civilized people everywhere. The trouble with Judaism was that it was very ancient, over a thousand years old, and its law, though well adapted perhaps to the needs of a primitive desert people, was often meaningless to a sophisticated, increasingly urban, and commercial community in the first century AD—and a huge and daily burden. It had never been fundamentally reformed and was administered and enforced by priests and scribes who constituted closed elites, whose jobs were often hereditary, and who resisted change with fanaticism. They were also quite capable of placing themselves in cynical alliance with the Roman authorities to prevent reformers from arousing the multitudes.

Judaism in the time of Jesus, then, was ripe for reformation like Christendom in the early sixteenth century. The question was: should it take violent and secular form to restore the Jewish kingdom as it had existed under David and the Maccabees? That is what some of the fundamentalist Jewish sects, such as the Essenes and the Zealots, advocated. They were eventually to get the upper hand in Jewish opinion a generation after Jesus's death, leading to the Great Revolt and the destruction of Jerusalem. The alternative was a spiritual revolution, the replacement of the unreformed law of Moses by a New Testament based on love and neighborliness, which could be embraced by all classes and all peoples.

That was the idea toward which Jesus's cousin John, son of Elizabeth, was moving. He had seen a vision in youth, and he knew that he had a special task to perform. To prepare himself he had lived for many years in the desert and adapted to it. He "was clothed with camel's hair, and with a girdle of a skin about his loins; and he did eat locusts and wild honey" (Mk 1:6). All four evangelists knew a lot about John, recognized his importance in the life of Jesus, and gave space to his mission accordingly. It is likely they had a common source briefed either by John himself or by one of his closest disciples (Mk 1:2–9ff.; Mt 3:1–15; Lk 3:2–22; Jn 1:6–34). John was essentially a humble man. He knew he was not the Christ, who the prophets foretold would come as a savior and a redeemer. He repeated many times the words of Isaiah: "I am the voice of one crying in the wilderness, Make straight the way of the Lord." He knew that the Christ was coming: "He it is," he said, "who coming after me is preferred before me, whose shoe's latchet I am not worthy to unloose."

John preached that in order to prepare for the Christ and the New Order all must come to him by the banks of the Jordan River and be immersed in it. This act of baptism, as he called it, was necessary to wash off the sins and habits of the past and thereby become a new man. But he recognized that his action was more symbolic than real, and that it required the godly power of the Christ himself to effect the inner transformation. John always insisted on this and made no miraculous claims for himself. All the same, he attracted huge crowds, and the attention of the authorities. According to the Gospel of John

(1:19–27), they "sent priests and Levites from Jerusalem to ask him, Who art thou? And he confessed, and denied not; but confessed, I am not the Christ. . . . I baptize with water: but there standeth one among you, whom ye know not." He then expressed his image of humility—"whose shoe's latchet I am not worthy to unloose."

The closeness of the various evangelical descriptions to one another, and the repetition of the Baptist's words, make it clear we are dealing with eyewitness accounts, probably more than one. The Gospel of John continues even more dramatically: "The next day John seeth Jesus coming unto him, and saith: Behold the Lamb of God, which taketh away the sin of the world" (1:29). According to the account the eyewitness gave to Matthew (3:14–17), John said to Jesus: "I have need to be baptized of thee, and comest thou to me? And Jesus answering him said unto him, Suffer it to be so now: for thus it becometh us to fulfil all righteousness." John then baptized Jesus, and when he came out of the water, "lo, the heavens were opened unto him, and he saw the Spirit of God descending like a dove, and lighting upon him: And lo a voice from heaven, saying, This is my beloved Son, in whom I am well pleased." According to Luke, one eyewitness reported, "the Holy Ghost descended in a bodily shape like a dove upon him" (3:22). Whether the dove was real or figurative, all four accounts agree on the essentials, that the baptism of Jesus was an extraordinary event, in which the presence of God was visual and audible, and witnessed by large crowds of men and women.

It may be asked: Why did Jesus need baptism? Was not the Son of God already prepared, in all respects, for his mission? This was John's own view, clearly. But Jesus was adamant that he must go through the ceremony of renewal. He was stressing the universality of the sacrament—the need for every human being to wash off the stains of the past and to become fresh, and new, and clean. It was the actual as well as the symbolic beginning of his New Testamental mission, which was to culminate in his institution of Communion in bread and wine—his own body and blood—at the Last Supper, immediately before his bodily sacrifice of the Crucifixion.

The baptism of Jesus was also the culmination of John's own mission. The third chapter of Luke gives details of John's preaching "the baptism of repentance and the remission of sins." It was rough and angry in content, adumbrating Jesus's warnings at their most fierce. When he recognized Pharisees and Sadducees among those seeking baptism, he shouted, "O generation of vipers, who hath warned you to flee from the wrath to come?" (Mt 3:7). He insisted that the Christ, when he came, would "throughly purge his floor, and gather his wheat into the garner; but he will burn up the chaff with unquenchable fire" (Mt 3:12). This was dangerous talk, and it was clearly reported to the higher religious authorities. This prepared the way for his arrest by Herod Antipas, the Roman puppet ruler of Galilee, who was already incensed by John's criticism of his incestuous marriage to Herodias, his brother's wife. She was not the granddaughter of Herod the Great for nothing. Once John was in her husband's dungeon, she incited her daughter Salome to dance lasciviously at a feast. Antipas was so enraptured he promised her, as a reward, anything in his power. Coached by her mother, she demanded the head of the Baptist, and her stepfather, though reluctant, complied. This dreadful event filled many pious Jews, who had heard John preach, with horror and fear. To Jesus it was another reminder, like the massacre of the innocents and the murder of Zacharias, of the danger of his mission; it brought home the unbridled brutality of the secular world, whose agents were available at any moment to destroy those ready to do God's work, and even those involved in it by accident. It was another admonitory prelude to death on the cross.

Immediately after Jesus was baptized, as part of the preparation for his ministry, he went into the wilderness. All three of the synoptic Gospels mention this episode, saying he went there at the bidding of the Holy Spirit (Mk 1:12–13; Mt 4:1–11; Lk 4:1–12). Mark's account is perfunctory, but both Matthew and Luke describe the experience in detail. He went into the wilderness—the wild country east of the Jordan—primarily to pray. Jesus was a convivial man, as we are repeatedly shown by the Gospel accounts. But he was also a prayerful man. When convivial he was emphatically a man. But when praying, he spoke directly with God, his Father, and necessarily was himself divine. Hence he always preferred to be alone. He did not stand in prayer, as the Jews were accustomed to do. He knelt, as a symbol of submission to the Father's will. Prayer, for him, meant separation from his fellow men, an ascent into divinity, and, as such, symbolized by altitude. When praying he preferred to be on a hill or a mountain—as he was in his Transfiguration (as we shall see), on the Mount of Olives in the Garden of Gethsemane before his Passion, and on the high mountain where he said his last prayers on earth before ascending into heaven.

So in the wilderness, praying, Jesus sought height for solitude. He fasted for forty days. We do not know the severity of his abstention from food and water. But Matthew and Luke insist that he was faint and hungry. Then, when his body was weak, came temptation, not just in his mind but in the bodily shape of Satan. It is not the only occasion when Jesus admitted he was tempted. He was so again at Gethsemane. When appalled at the enormity of the suffering immediately ahead of him, he prayed to his Father that it be lifted, then submitted. In the wilderness, however, the struggle was not in his mind but in the open, with Satan visible, vocal, and formidable in power. The fact that Jesus recounted the details afterward to his followers shows how anxious he was to impress upon them that evil is not merely objective and material but also subjective and personal; that Satan exists and has to be overcome by strength of will and clearness of distinction between the good and the bad. He transformed his personal temptation into a universal experience.

For Jesus himself the temptation was to use his divine powers for earthly material purposes: first, to turn stones into bread; then, to preserve his life from mortal dangers; finally, to possess the world. The third temptation (here I am following Matthew's account) was the most serious because of its universal scope: it applied not only to such as himself, endowed with divine powers, but also to mankind, who, thanks to high intelligence and industry, can acquire vast powers which—superficially at least—appear godlike. Jesus told Matthew's apostolic source that on this third occasion Satan "taketh him up into an exceeding high mountain, and sheweth him all the kingdoms of the world, and the glory of them; And saith unto him, All these things will I give thee, if thou wilt fall down and worship me" (4:8–9).

The "high mountain" is significant—the constant image when Jesus is about to perceive important truths—as is the plural reference to "kingdoms." The temptation concerns not just states and empires but knowledge—kingdoms of the mind, science—the understanding of the universe by physics and mathematics and of the human body by Darwinian evolution, by biology, and by the chromosomal structure, and the explosion of human penetration, in all distinctions, of the secrets of the universe. Here was the most insidious of all temptations: that men obtain huge victories of the intellect by agreeing to worship material success and to renounce the world of the spirit, to put knowledge before goodness and mastery of the elements before their Creator.

Jesus said that there was only one possible reply to this final temptation: "Get thee hence, Satan: for it is written, Thou shalt worship the Lord thy God, and him only shalt thou serve" (4:10). Pride in knowledge, pride in the human capacity to acquire it—at the expense of ignoring God—is just another form of idolatry. Thus dismissed, Satan departed, leaving Jesus alone, "and, behold, angels came and ministered unto him" (4:11).

So Jesus returned from the wilderness uncorrupted and, as a man, wiser and more experienced. He was ready to begin. What sort of a man was he? We are not told. His precursor, the Baptist, is described. But not once, in all the four Gospels, are we given any indication of Jesus's appearance. Nor are we told what he looked like in any of the canonical epistles or any documents of the first century AD. It is not until well into the second century, by which time the chain of oral eyewitness evidence had long been broken, that we get the first iconography, and these attempts are typology rather than actual portraiture. The Jesus who then appears is a beardless figure of ideal character. There are 104 examples in the catacombs, 97 in sarcophagi, 14 in mosaics, 45 in gold glasses, 50 in other artifacts, and 3 in manuscripts. Later he appears as a grown man, bearded but still idealized: and this Jesus, suitably rendered human, is the man who thereafter is painted and sculpted by artists in the Western tradition. But the earliest appearance of the bearded Jesus dates from centuries after his death. In short, there is no reliable evidence of what Jesus looked like.

On the other hand, we know certain things about his visual personality which struck eyewitnesses and so are recorded in the Gospels. Jesus was very observant. It is notable how many times he is described as "looking," "looking upon," "looking round," "looking up" (the last is mentioned three times). His habit of penetrating observation punctuates the narrative: "[H]e looked round" before speaking. "And he lifted up his eyes on his disciples and said . . ." "And the Lord turned, and looked upon Peter." "[H]e had looked round about on them with anger, being grieved for the hardness of their hearts." He was a man greatly interested in detail. He missed nothing. He had a penetrating gaze, which eyewitnesses noticed and remembered. His all-seeing eyes were, almost certainly, the first thing that struck people about him.

His gaze was linked to his air of decision. It astonished people. He appeared and spoke not as an interpreter of the scriptures but as a fountainhead of truth. Matthew makes this clear: "For he taught them as one having authority, and not as the scribes" (7:29). Moreover, the authority he exercised was there from the beginning of his ministry. He did not need to acquire it. It was innate. In the light of what followed, we can see it was divine. Being God, he had no need to scrabble about among the texts and commentaries: he was the truth incarnate. But he was man, too, visibly and obviously, and therefore his air of authority struck observers, from the very first day, as arresting. He was man, and he needed to be man, for four reasons: First, to put people to the test of faith. Second, to communicate as a human being. Third, to suffer. And fourth, to serve as a model for all time, which he could do only as man—"the way of Jesus." And, being a man, he needed helpers, disciples, apostles.

The choosing of the apostles, the first important act of Jesus's ministry, is variously described by the evangelists (Mt 4:18ff.; Mk 1:16ff.; Lk 5:3ff.; Jn 1:38ff.). Luke says that after the wilderness experience Jesus began to preach, alone, in Galilee, his home territory, where there were well over one hundred small towns and villages, many with synagogues. In one (according to Luke 4:18ff.) he was given the book of Isaiah, and he read from it: "The spirit of the Lord is upon me, . . . to preach the gospel to the poor; he hath sent me to heal the brokenhearted, to preach deliverance to the captives, and the

recovering of sight to the blind, to set at liberty them that are
bruised." When he closed the book and handed it back to the
priest, he sat down. "And the eyes of all them that were in the
synagogue were fastened on him." So he continued to talk
while sitting. And they all "wondered at the gracious words
which proceeded out of his mouth. And they said, Is not this
Joseph's son?" But Jesus determined to tell them things they
did not wish to hear. He quoted the proverb "Physician, heal
thyself" and noted, "No prophet is accepted in his own country." He went on to criticize Elias and Eliseus and to remind the
congregation of the limitations of their power. His listeners
were outraged. "[W]hen they heard these things, [they] were
filled with wrath, And rose up, and thrust him out of the city,
and led him unto the brow of the hill whereon their city was
built, that they might cast him down headlong." He was obliged
to exercise his miraculous powers: "But he passing through the
midst of them went his way."

He went to Capernaum, on the Sea of Galilee, and it was
there that he chose his first followers, sturdy fishermen, strong
and resourceful, to stand around him and protect him when
his words angered the self-righteously orthodox. According to
the fifth chapter of Luke, he taught the people from Simon
Peter's fishing boat, which was close to the shore while Simon
was washing his nets, having toiled all night in vain. To thank
Simon he performed a minor miracle. He told him: "Launch

out into the deep, and let down your nets for a draught." Despite having caught nothing in this spot, Simon did as he was bid, and "they inclosed a great multitude of fishes: and their net brake." They called their partners, James and John, sons of Zebedee, and together they took so many fish aboard that their boats began to sink. Simon fell down at Jesus's knees, saying, "Depart from me; for I am a sinful man, O Lord." Jesus replied, "Fear not; from henceforth thou shalt catch men." Luke adds: "And when they had brought their ships to land, they forsook all, and followed him."

John has another version of this choosing which concerns Andrew, Simon's brother. He and another man are described as "disciples" of the Baptist. When they heard the Baptist say of Jesus, "Behold the Lamb of God," they followed him and asked, "Master, where dwelleth thou?" He said, "Come and see." They did and stayed with him, and then Andrew got hold of Simon and told him, "We have found the Messiah." It was when Simon was introduced to Jesus that he was renamed Peter, meaning a stone or rock. Matthew again varies the tale by having Jesus say to Simon and Andrew, "Follow me, and I will make you fishers of men." Mark uses the same phrase and says that, thus accompanied by the four stalwart fishermen, Jesus went into Capernaum and began teaching in the synagogue "straightway on the sabbath." The fact that Andrew was a disciple of the Baptist suggests to me that the little group of fishermen who worked together were already hovering on the brink of religious revivalism. But Andrew was only a part-time follower of John. Jesus insisted that the group come with him full-time, and they obeyed. The sons of Zebedee, Mark says, "left their father Zebedee in the ship with the hired servants."

Jesus was adamant that the men he called must put the mission first. In a striking passage in Matthew (10:34–38) he admitted that his work would cause dissension within families: "[A]nd a man's foes shall be they of his own household." Sons against fathers, mothers against daughters, mothers-in-law against daughters-in-law. Although he called only men for public purposes, the fact that he mentions the womenfolk shows that he also recruited women to sustain the mission in various ways and expected them to serve with equal devotion—as, indeed, they did. In this difficult and hard-edged passage, Jesus stresses the absolutist nature of a vocation to serve him. It involved painful choices. "He that loveth father and mother more than me is not worthy of me: and he that loveth son or daughter more than me is not worthy of me. And he that taketh not his cross, and followeth after me, is not worthy of me."

The reference to the cross is significant. Jesus had just narrowly escaped death at the hands of angry bigots, and was never in any doubt about the danger of his mission. His launching of it coincided with—may have been accelerated by—the arrest of the Baptist. Andrew may not have been the only follower of the Baptist among the apostles, and certainly many were soon recruited among the mass of Jesus's disciples. But Jesus cast his net wide, and though the core of his apostles were fishermen, he deliberately chose men of diverse occupations, including those who were anathema to the orthodox, such as tax collectors, or publicans as they were known. At the north end of the Sea of Galilee was a road from Damascus to Acre on the Mediterranean. At the boundary between the territory of Philip the Tetrarch and Herod Antipas, ruler of the area where Jesus was operating, was a customhouse, where tolls were exacted on goods passing along the road. Jesus passed it, saw Matthew sitting inside counting, and said to him, "Follow me." As he said the words, the penetrating look in his eyes, as they met Matthew's, is the subject of one of Caravaggio's greatest paintings, now on display at the Contarelli Chapel in Rome. Matthew obeyed instantly.

Not all of those whom Jesus called responded. One of the saddest stories in the Gospels occurs in Mark 10:17–22. On the Judaean coast, a man came running up to him and knelt at his feet. He asked, "[W]hat shall I do that I may inherit eternal life?" Jesus listed the commandments, and the man replied, "[A]ll these have I observed from my youth." Jesus felt a flash of deep affection for this earnest believer and "beholding him loved him." So he decided to call him, too, and said, "[S]ell whatsoever thou hast, and give to the poor, and thou shalt have treasure in heaven: and come, take up the cross, and follow me." But the man felt it was asking too much: "And he was sad at that saying, and went away grieved: for he had great possessions."

The twelve apostles were enlisted early in Jesus's ministry, and all three synoptics give their names (Lk 6:13–16; Mt 10:2–4; Mk 3:14–19). Luke's list is Simon Peter and his brother Andrew; James and John, brothers whom Jesus called "the Sons of Thunder" because of their enthusiasm; Philip, the cautious one; Bartholomew (referred to as Nathanael, his other name, in John); Matthew; Thomas (later "Doubting Thomas"); James, the son of Alphaeus; Simon, known as the Zealot; Judas, brother of James; and Judas Iscariot. In the lists given by Matthew and Mark, Simon the Zealot is given as "the Canaanite," and Thaddaeus is included instead of the first Judas. But Thaddaeus and this Judas may be the same person: in first-century Palestine, many men had more than one name, often a Greek name (like Andrew or Philip) as well as an Aramaic one, and some like Nathanael were called after their father. Bearing this in mind, the close conjunction of the lists is remarkable. It is likely, in my view, that all early Christians knew the names of the apostles, in order, by heart.

The twelve were special. They had particular functions and were given powers to carry them out. Mark says Jesus "ordained" them close to a high place, as was his custom, to begin the Christian priesthood, the "apostolic succession," as it came to be called, which continues to this day, two thousand years later: "And he goeth up into a mountain, and calleth unto him whom he would: and they came unto him . . . that he might send them forth to preach" (3:13–14).

Thus was Jesus's mission prepared for and organized. What was its object? At whom was it aimed? And what were its methods?

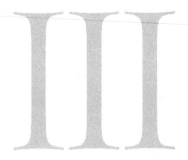

✝ The Danger of the Miracles

I N CHOOSING HIS APOSTLES, Jesus astonished them by the way in which he identified them, and by his knowledge of their lives. It led Nathanael, in John's account, to hail him as "the Son of God . . . the King of Israel" (1:49). Jesus replied that he seemed easily impressed: "[T]hou shalt see greater things than these" (1:50). But it is important to note that Jesus, conscious as he was of supernatural powers of every kind, was unwilling to use them for display—that was one of the temptations he resisted in the wilderness. He was a reluctant miracle worker.

Three days after he chose his first apostles, as John relates, he attended a wedding at the town of Cana, not far from the shores of the Sea of Galilee, where his fishermen disciples worked. They went with him. It was a family affair. A member of his mother's numerous clan was getting married. John's account (2:1–11) of what he calls the "beginning of miracles" is one of the most fascinating episodes in the entire New Testament, proving as it does the authenticity of the account and its detailed accuracy. At the very least, it illuminates the intimacy between Jesus and his mother, her ability to read his mind.

Mary was anxious because Jesus had brought so many of his followers with him. Whether because of the extra uninvited, though welcome, guests, or for reasons not disclosed— mismanagement, as common in the first century AD as it is today—the wine ran out. Mary, concerned about the shame this would bring on her family, expected Jesus to do something about it. She told him, "They have no wine." Her calm expectation that he would perform a miracle for a purely social purpose shows she was already fully aware of his powers. But her presumption brought a sharp retort: "Woman, what have I to do with thee? mine hour is not yet come." From everything we know about him, it is impossible to see Jesus being rude to his mother—to anyone, indeed, but to her least of all. Certainly, that is not how Mary took his reply. With her instinctive maternal knowledge of his goodness and devotion to her, she interpreted his apparent refusal to help as a sure sign he would do what she wished. So she said calmly to the servants, "Whatsoever he saith unto you, do it."

Now comes the second detail which speaks truth. Jesus noticed six huge pots of stone, empty now but usually containing "two or three firkins apiece" (a firkin was eight gallons). He told the servants to fill them up with water, and when they had done so, he ordered, "Draw out now, and bear unto the governor of the feast." And now comes the third detail which conveys verisimilitude. The master of ceremonies (or "governor"), of a type that happily no longer exists—at least in the West—felt it incumbent on his dignity to pronounce on the quality of the wine. He told the bridegroom, "Every man at the beginning doth set forth good wine; and when men have well drunk, then that which is worse: but thou hast kept the good wine until now." One wonders what this self-important person could have said, in rebuke, if Mary and Jesus had permitted the wine to run out. As it was, Jesus had provided, by my calculations, nearly a thousand bottles of vintage quality. This was talked about among the drinking classes of northeast Galilee, the men terming it "glory." The details of the new supply we may take to be correct, for where alcohol is concerned men rarely make statistical mistakes.

Cana, as it happens, was not the first miracle. For one had already occurred to enable Jesus to escape being murdered by the pious mob at the hilltop synagogue, and another when Jesus raised the draught of fish when calling Simon Peter and his colleagues. But all three miracles were reluctant, a response by Jesus to a situation rather than a deliberate use of his supernatural powers to impress.

Indeed, though working miracles was regarded as one of the most notable aspects of Jesus's ministry at the time and ever since, Jesus did not place much importance on it. Twenty years after his death, St. Paul distinguishes between Hebrew and Greek culture: "For the Jews require a sign, and the Greeks seek after wisdom" (1 Cor 1:22). In Jewish theology, God created nature, which itself was a miracle, or an unending series of miracles. And God's decision to suspend nature on a particular occasion was another kind of miracle that punctuates the Old Testament as a sign of his power. Jesus was always prepared to demonstrate God's power by miracle, when it was necessary to do so. But he repeatedly rejected the mere role of miracle worker as a human instrument of "signs and wonders." Luke says he regarded the incessant clamor of the people for "signs" as itself the sign of "an evil generation": "[T]hey seek a sign; and there shall no sign be given it" (11:29). And in telling the story of Lazarus the beggar and the wicked rich man (Lk 16:19–31) Jesus makes it clear that it is preferable in God's eyes that men show faith by listening to the holy truth, and by accepting it and following it, rather than by waiting for signs and miracles to convince them. Jesus taught that the truth was reasonable, that goodness made sense, that to follow his teaching and obey God's commandments was a rational thing to do. Hence he was much closer to the Greek position than to the Jewish one. St. Paul's work in giving Jesus's message in terms of Greek culture was thus carrying out the Master's intention, and St. Thomas Aquinas's great theological structure in his thirteenth-century *Summa theologica*, showing Christianity as the moral architecture of reason, was the intellectual culmination of a process which Jesus began in Galilee twelve centuries before.

Nevertheless, Jesus performed miracles. I have counted dozens of occasions recorded by the evangelists in which they occurred. Three of them were multiple healings of the sick and exorcisms of those possessed by devils. The others concerned either individuals or incidents when Jesus interrupted the normal course of nature by stilling a tempest or causing a fig tree to wither. The evangelists record the miracles in different ways. Mark, reflecting the memories of St. Peter, who always reacted dramatically to miracles, records eighteen of them: indeed, his brief text is virtually an account of Jesus's miracle ministry. Matthew's much longer text records twenty, but he devotes most of his space to what Jesus said: his is essentially the "teaching Gospel." Luke also notes twenty miracles, but he stresses the secondary place they occupied in Jesus's work. Also the author of the Acts of the Apostles, he tries to show that mere men, the apostles, could perform healing miracles of exactly the same kind as Jesus himself did—one need not be the Son of God to exercise this derivative or vicarious power. Thus Luke's account in Acts 9:32–42 shows Peter duplicating Jesus's work in curing the paralytic Aeneas (Lk 5:18–26) and raising

Dorcas (Lk 8:49–56). John records only nine miracles, though these include the Cana beginning and the most significant miracle of all, the raising of Lazarus from the dead when his body was already decomposing (11:1–44), which prefigures his own Resurrection. The only occasion when all evangelists record the same miracle is when Jesus fed the five thousand.

On most occasions when Jesus consented to perform a miracle, his motive was compassion. His heart went out to the sick, the infirm, the stricken, especially if they were old and had suffered the burden of incapacity for many years. When teaching to a synagogue, Jesus noticed an old woman in a pitiable state who "had a spirit of infirmity eighteen years, and was bowed together, and could in no wise lift up herself. And when Jesus saw her, he called her to him, and said unto her, Woman, thou are loosed from thine infirmity. And he laid his hands on her: and immediately she was made straight, and glorified God" (Lk 13:11–13). Here was Jesus the perceptive: noticing a dreadful case of debility in a crowded congregation and acting swiftly. More often, in the press of the crowds, it was the friends of the sick, or the sick themselves, who begged him to do something. Near Decapolis, the friends of a deaf and dumb man brought him to Jesus and "beseech[ed] him to put his hand upon him." Jesus "took him aside" and "put his fingers into his ears, and he spit, and touched his tongue." Jesus then sighed, and said in Aramaic, "Be opened." The man's ears were immediately opened, "and the string of his tongue was loosed, and he spake plain." This was another case of compassion and, far from making it a "sign," Jesus "charged them that they should tell no man." But the more he insisted on silent gratitude, "the more a great deal they published it" (Mk 7:32–36).

Jesus gave little credit to those whose faith was inspired by a miracle he performed. He was more impressed by those who already had faith that he could perform one. Matthew (8:5–13) and Luke (7:1–10) tell the touching story of a Roman officer, a centurion, who came up to him in Capernaum and beseeched him: "Lord, my servant lieth at home sick of the palsy, grievously tormented." Jesus's heart always warmed to those who cared for their underlings as well as their families, and immediately he said he would come and heal the servant. But the officer had complete faith in Jesus's mere words. He explained, "I am a man under authority, having soldiers under me: and I say to this man, Go, and he goeth; and to another, Come, and he cometh; and to my servant, Do this, and he doeth it." He explained that he was not worthy that Jesus "shouldest come under my roof." All he asked for was a command which he knew would be obeyed: "[S]peak the word only and my servant shall be healed." This was the true kind of faith Jesus was looking for. He said to the crowd, "Verily I say unto you, I have not found so great faith, no, not in Israel." He took the occasion to warn that many who believed themselves chosen deluded themselves, and that the great mass of the saved should be drawn from "east and west"—making it clear that his mission was not just to the Jews but, above all, to the Gentiles, or to humanity as a whole. Matthew and Luke tell this significant story in almost identical words and insist the centurion's orderly was healed from the hour Jesus spoke.

Jesus had no way to prevent this miracle from being talked about, and no doubt it caused a stir. As a rule, however, when moved by compassion to cure, he took trouble that no one knew. In Bethsaida, a blind man was brought to him by his friends, who "besought [Jesus] to touch him." Jesus "took the blind man by the hand," separated him from his friends, "and led him out of the town." Finally when they were alone he "put his hands upon him" and "asked him if he saw ought." The man said, "I see men as trees, walking." Jesus then again put his hands on the man's eyes and asked him to describe what he saw. This time he "saw every man clearly." So Jesus sent him home by himself, saying, "Neither go into the town, nor tell it to any in the town" (Mk 8:22–26). It is notable that Jesus, moved by compassion and the faith of the suffering, preferred to cure the afflicted away from public view. When Jesus was in Nazareth, he was followed by two blind men who said, "Son of David, have mercy on us." He waited until they followed him into his house, and they were alone, when he said, "Believe ye that I am able to do this? They said unto him:

Yea, Lord. Then touched he their eyes, saying, According to your faith be it unto you. And their eyes were opened; and Jesus straitly charged them, saying, See that no man know it" (Mt 9:27–30).

Of course, the blind men, thus cured, could not resist telling everyone all about it. But Jesus was always anxious to show that a mere miracle of healing the sick was only a superficial proof of God's enormous powers given to him. Earlier that same day in Nazareth, "they brought to him a man sick of the palsy, lying on a bed." Jesus told him, "[B]e of good cheer; thy sins be forgiven thee." Some scribes who were watching said to themselves, "This man blasphemeth." Jesus, guessing their thoughts, said, "Wherefore think ye evil in your hearts? For whether is easier, to say, Thy sins be forgiven thee; or to say, Arise, and walk? But that ye may know that the Son of man hath power on earth to forgive sins, (then saith he to the sick of the palsy,) Arise, take up thy bed, and go unto thine house." According to Matthew, "he arose, and departed to his house" (9:2–7). On occasions when Jesus deliberately sought witnesses to a miracle, his aim was to expose the bigotry of his orthodox critics. It was one of their tenets that even to perform a miracle on the Sabbath day was sinful, since it was work, albeit with God's power. At the opening of Mark's third chapter, he says that Jesus entered a synagogue and found a man with a withered hand. The Pharisees were watching, waiting for him to heal the man, so that they could accuse him of breaking the Sabbath. Jesus told the man, "Stand forth." Then he asked the Pharisees, "Is it lawful to do good on the sabbath days, or to do evil? to save life or to kill?" They refused to answer. Jesus "looked round about on them with anger, being grieved for the hardness of their hearts." He told the man to stretch out his hand, and when he did so it "was restored whole as the other." The Pharisees left to report not the miracle but the breach of the Sabbath and the provocative behavior of Jesus. They "straightway took counsel with the Herodians against him, how they might destroy him" (3:1–6).

The fact is, as Jesus knew from the start, invoking God's power through miracles, whether successfully or not, was dangerous in a country prone to religious hysteria, where the authorities, both secular and ecclesiastical, were determined to stamp out what they could not control or make use of for their own purposes. The high priests, the scribes, and the organized sects like the Pharisees were not convinced of Jesus's sanctity by his cures. They suspected trickery, or collusion with the "sick," or worse, the work of evil spirits. When Jesus cured disturbed people, believed to be possessed by devils, they accused him of working with Beelzebub, the prince of devils.

Nor was the hostility of the powerful the only risk Jesus faced. The fact that he could cure chronically sick people led to riotous behavior among those seeking relief and their anxious friends and families. When Jesus entered a place in Capernaum, and "it was noised that he was in the house," a huge crowd collected, so that there was no room within. A man sick of the palsy, evidently wealthy, since he had four attendants who carried him around, came to the house, but his men could not get him in because of what Mark calls "the press" of the crowds. So, desperate and excited, "they uncovered the roof" of the house where Jesus was, "and when they had broken it up, they let down the bed wherein the sick of the palsy lay" (2:1–4). This was the occasion when Jesus forgave the sick man his sins, thus scandalizing the orthodox, before telling him to take up his bed and walk. The Pharisees were furious—and the man who owned the house cannot have been too pleased either.

A similar, but even more striking, tale of the inconveniences of miracles is given in Matthew 8:28–34 about the region around Gadara, east of the Sea of Galilee. Matthew came from this part of the country and therefore was able to identify the actual town, Gergesa, on cliffs overlooking the water, where the incident occurred. There, two men possessed by devils who lived among the tombs (one described as "exceeding fierce") recognized and confronted Jesus. The devils begged him, if he should cast them out of the men, to permit them to go into a herd of swine that was feeding peacefully nearby. Jesus consented. The devils left the men and "went into the herd of swine: and, behold, the whole herd of swine ran violently down a steep place into the sea, and perished in the waters." The herdsmen, terrified, "went their ways into the city, and told every thing." Matthew, for whom the incident was only too familiar, concludes: "And, behold, the whole city came out to meet Jesus: and when they saw him, they besought him that he would depart out of their coasts." As one would expect. The ways of a miracle worker were hard.

Indeed, as his ministry continued, Jesus increasingly avoided working miracles, except when entreated in such a way that he could not refuse. The fifth chapter of Mark (22–43) tells us about two of these cases. On the northwest side of the Sea of Galilee, the area where Jesus was best known, a prominent Jew called Jairus, "one of the rulers of the synagogue," who had helped him to preach there, "fell at his feet, And besought him greatly." He said his twelve-year-old daughter "lieth at the point of death." He begged Jesus to "come and lay thy hands on her, that she may be healed." Jesus went with him but was "thronged" by the mob. An old woman saw her opportunity to get his help. Hers was a pitiful tale. She had suffered for twelve years from "an issue of blood," a common postmenstrual complaint, in an acute form. She had meekly put up with the fruitless efforts of many doctors, who had taken all her money in fees, "and was nothing bettered, but rather grew worse." She had heard of Jesus, joined the crowd, and in the press of bodies contrived to touch his garment: "For she said, If I may touch but his clothes, I shall be whole." And it was true: "[S]traightway the fountain of her blood was dried up; and she felt in her body that she was healed of that plague." But Jesus felt it, too, "immediately knowing in himself that virtue had gone out of him." Turning round in the crowd, he asked, "Who touched my clothes?" The disciples were puzzled. In that immense, pressing throng, how could anyone possibly tell? But the woman heard, and knew. "[F]earing and trembling," she fell down before Jesus and told him the truth. He looked with kindness on her. Seeing she was old and trembling, he did not address her with the formal "Woman," but said, "Daughter, thy faith hath made thee whole; go in peace."

Meanwhile, one of Jairus's family arrived to tell him there was no point in troubling Jesus further: the little girl was dead. But Jesus insisted on going to Jairus's house. There he found a crowd of relatives, servants, and minstrels performing the funeral dirge—"making a noise" as Matthew puts it (9:23). He commanded silence, saying, "[T]he maid is not dead, but sleepeth" (9:24). He ordered them all out of the house and, accompanied only by the girl's parents, Peter, James, and John, went into the room where she lay (Lk 8:51). "[H]e took the damsel by the hand, and said unto her, Talitha cumi," a phrase in Aramaic meaning "Little girl, get up" (Mk 5:41). The girl arose and walked. Then comes the small detail that lends touching authenticity to the story. Jesus loved children and understood them. The little girl had been given nothing to eat while she lay in mortal sickness and the doctors fussed around her bed. Now she was up, and Jesus knew she must be hungry. Luke says that his first instruction was that she must be given something to eat.

But his next was to command all those people present that they say nothing. As always, he wanted to avoid at all costs being known as a miracle worker. He detested being thought of as a kind of holy magician. In none of the four Gospels is there a single instance of his using his powers of healing to attract support—just the opposite. But sometimes publicity was unavoidable, and it could be dangerous, as well as irksome, to a profoundly thoughtful man and speaker who was eager to convey his message by reason and not by "signs." It became clear, as his mission proceeded, that the Jewish authorities were increasingly anxious to destroy or at least to silence him. To them, the fact that he had unusual powers was an added reason to eliminate an outsider who challenged their authority. For them, the crisis became acute when it was shown he had power to wield. This point is made particularly clear by John in his Gospel, which is the only one to describe the raising of Jesus's friend Lazarus (11:1–57).

We are told that Jesus was very fond of Lazarus, though we do not know why, for he never speaks in the Gospel accounts and is not strongly characterized like his sisters Martha and Mary. They lived in the town of Bethany, on the eastern slopes of the Mount of Olives, to the east of Jerusalem. Jesus had other friends there besides Lazarus and his sisters, and often stayed there when visiting Jerusalem. But he was watched there as a suspicious character "known" to the Temple authorities, who once raised a mob to stone him out of the town. John 11 describes how, toward the end of his ministry, while Jesus and his companions were over the border in Samaria, messengers arrived from Martha and Mary to say that Lazarus was sick. Jesus waited two days, then announced he was crossing into Judaea to go to Bethany. He explained, "This sickness is not unto death, but for the glory of God, that the Son of God may be glorified thereby." But, after delaying for two days, for reasons which are a mystery to us, he announced that Lazarus was dead: "And I am glad for your sakes that I was not there, to the intent ye may believe; nevertheless let us go unto him." The disciples said, "Master, the Jews of late sought to stone thee; and goest thou thither again?" Thomas, known as Didymus, believed Jesus was going to his death, and said to his comrades: "Let us also go, that we may die with him."

When they arrived, Jesus found Lazarus had not only died but been put in his tomb four days before. The town was full of Jews who had come out from Jerusalem to console Martha and Mary, for Lazarus was obviously a popular and highly esteemed person. Mary stayed in the house, weeping. But Martha came out to meet Jesus, and the following conversation took place.

MARTHA: Lord, if thou hadst been here, my brother had not died. But I know, that even now, whatsoever thou wilt ask of God, God will give it thee.

JESUS: Thy brother shall rise again.

MARTHA: I know that he shall rise again in the resurrection of the last day.

JESUS: I am the resurrection, and the life: he that believeth in me, though he were dead, yet shall he live: And whosoever liveth and believeth in me shall never die. Believest thou this?

MARTHA: Yea, Lord: I believe that thou art the Christ, the Son of God, which should come into the world.

Then she went home and called her sister Mary "secretly" and said, "The Master is come, and calleth for thee." Mary immediately ran to where Jesus was waiting outside the town. The Jews from the house followed her, saying, "She goeth unto the grave to weep there." Mary, seeing Jesus, knelt at his feet, and said, "Lord, if thou hadst been here, my brother had not died." She wept, and the Jews with her wept. Jesus "groaned in the spirit, and was troubled." He said, "Where have ye laid him?" and they replied, "[C]ome and see." John adds: "Jesus wept." The Jews said, "Behold how he loved him." But others said, "Could not this man, which opened the eyes of the blind, have caused that even this man should not have died?" Jesus groaned again, until they came to the tomb, a cave blocked by a stone. He said, "Take ye away the stone." Martha, always the direct and practical one, warned him, "Lord, by this time he stinketh: for he has been dead four days." Jesus reminded her that if she believed she would see the glory of God. Then the stone was lifted up, and Jesus raised his eyes to heaven, saying, "Father, I thank thee that thou hast heard me." In a loud voice he cried, "Lazarus, come forth." Lazarus did so, "bound hand and foot with graveclothes: and his face was bound about with a napkin." Jesus said, "Loose him, and let him go."

This was by far the greatest of Jesus's miracles. There was no way he could avoid it and no way it could be kept private, according to his rule. It was witnessed by many pious Jews, some of whom were converted on the spot and were sure now that Jesus was the Son of God. But others went back to Jerusalem and complained to the Pharisees and to the Temple authorities that some kind of devilry was taking place, and soon there would be rioting. The chief priests called a council meeting. They asked one another, "What do we? for this man doeth many miracles. If we let him thus alone, all men will believe on him: and the Romans shall come and take away both our place and nation."

The chief priest for the year, Caiaphas, was scornful: "Ye know nothing at all." He said it was expedient that "one man should die for the people" and that Jesus was the appointed man: "Then from that day forth they took counsel together for to put him to death." In this account John showed the double-edged effect that miracles had—only Jesus's own attitude to them was so ambiguous. Miracles convinced the people that Jesus was a special person, but they also aroused the hostility of the Jewish authorities. Despite the truth of the miracles—indeed, precisely because they believed, or half-believed, in them—the priests, the scribes, the Pharisees and other pious and orthodox observant Jews decided Jesus was a threat both to them personally and to the Jewish community. It was the miracles, and their obvious success and truth, which persuaded these men to put Jesus to death. For they drew attention to the real threat—Jesus's teaching, which promised to overthrow all their traditional, ancient, exclusive, and hieratic values. What they really feared was what they saw looming: a new moral world. To that we now turn.

IV

✝ What Jesus Taught and Why

JESUS TAUGHT for the best part of three years in south-east Galilee and Jerusalem. His early ministry centered on Capernaum, on the Sea of Galilee, with visits to Jerusalem and parts of Samaria. During his central ministry he made a first tour of Galilee, visiting Nazareth and other towns. Then followed trips to the eastern shores of the Sea of Galilee and a second tour of Galilee villages. A third tour of Galilee also included visits beyond it to Tyre and Sidon, Decapolis, Caesarea, and Philippi. In his late ministry, he was in Peraea, parts of Judaea, and Galilee again, until his triumphal entry into Jerusalem that led to his arrest and Crucifixion.

The ministry was continual. Even when he traveled, Jesus taught by the wayside. There is no evidence he preached formal sermons, let alone regular, repeated ones. Indeed, the word "preached" should not be used about him. "Taught" is more accurate. He taught as the Holy Spirit moved him, often in response to what he saw or heard, or to questions. He used synagogues where those in charge of them were friendly, or he taught in the open. Jesus was not thus overburdened by a program of specific appointments to teach. While always at work, he gives the impression of finding time to chat, albeit not about trivialities. There is never a sense of hurry. Of course, Jesus, who was God as well as man, was partly outside the structure of time and space anyway. He could, and did, make time stand still, and he could annihilate the constraints of space. This was particularly true when he wished to pray, as he often did, outside time or upon a hill or mountain, beyond space. But when not praying, he was teaching, even at mealtimes, for Jesus was convivial and loved to teach when people were relaxed and enjoying their food and companionship. I calculate that Jesus, in his three-year ministry, must have taught on perhaps as many as four hundred occasions when crowds gathered, as well as scores of other times when an informal opportunity arose. His few rest days were spent fishing on the great lake around which his ministry revolved. The disciples fished, as they well knew how, while Jesus reclined in the stern and sometimes slept.

What did Jesus teach? He had no system, no summa, no code. God forbid! The only way to grasp his teaching is to read all the Gospels repeatedly, until its essence permeates the mind. In the ancient Near East, centuries before the birth of Christ, when societies were just emerging from savagery, religious awe and belief served to civilize by producing elaborate codes of law to preserve order, because there were no civil parliaments or constitutional bodies to perform this function. These religious codes were elaborated by layers of commentaries produced by professional priests, scribes, and ecclesiastical lawyers. This process was particularly intense among the Jews, who could trace their religious-legal roots back to Moses or even Abraham, and who had, by Jesus's time, already enjoyed a continuity and a progressive elaboration of legal duties stretching back two millennia. In the process, God had become a very distant and frightening figure, but the law was an ever-present and weighty reality.

Jesus was a revolutionary who transformed the entire Judaic religious scheme into something quite different. It ceased to be a penal system of law and punishment—that could be left to Caesar and his soldiers—and became an affair of the heart and an adventure of the spirit. Jesus did not exactly repudiate the law. What he did was to extract its moral code and ignore the rest. Instead of the law he spoke of the Kingdom of God or the Kingdom of Heaven. A faithful soul was not one who obeyed the law but one who, by transforming his spirit, "entered" the Kingdom. God was not a distant, terrifying Yahweh but "the Father."

Essentially, in Jesus's teaching, the entire human race was "the children of God." He used the term "Father" or "Holy Father" more often than any other. According to Luke 11:2–4, when a disciple asked him how to pray, Jesus taught him the words of the Our Father, or Lord's Prayer, an admirably succinct and intimate address to God, who is treated as the father of a close family rather than an invisible deity on a mountain. Later, on the eve of his Passion, in the Garden of Gethsemane, he prayed directly to God in an extended and transcendental version of the Our Father, which is given at full length in the seventeenth chapter of John. Jesus always taught that the present world, though created by God and good and beautiful in many respects, to be enjoyed and made use of within reason, was totally different from the Kingdom of God. It was alien, and human beings could never be fully at home in it. It was as though something in them, some vital part, was missing.

They needed to be "made whole." This process could not be achieved by obeying endless laws, or even by doing good works, meritorious though they were. It depended entirely on the mercy of God, whose son was the symbol and instrument by his sacrifice. Life on earth was to be devoted to a self-transformation in which each human soul strove to become as like God as possible, a process made easier by the existence of his son made man, thus facilitating imitation.

The essence of Jesus's teaching is the search for oneness. What matters is not the world, a mere episode in time and space, but the people in it: their sojourn in the world is temporary, and their object is to emerge from it and become one with God. About to depart the world, Jesus prayed to God for his faithful followers: "And now I am no more in the world, but these are in the world, and I come to thee. Holy Father, keep through thine own name those whom thou hast given me, that they may be one, as we are" (Jn 17:11).

In Jesus's eyes, the faithful are alien to the world: "[T]hey are not of the world, even as I am not of the world," a sentence so important he repeats it (Jn 17:14, 16). He adds (17:20–26):

> Neither pray I for these [followers] alone, but for them also which shall believe on me. . . . That they all may be one; as thou, Father, art in me, and I in thee, that they also may be one in us. . . . And the glory which thou gavest me I have given them; that they may be one, even as we are one: I in them, and thou in me, that they may be made perfect in one. . . . O righteous Father, the world hath not known thee: but I have known thee, and these have known that thou has sent me. And I have declared unto them thy name, and will declare it: that the love wherewith thou hast loved me may be in them, and I in them.

Jesus said this magnificent and intimate prayer while kneeling. Moses had taught the Hebrews to pray standing, and aloud,
with arms outstretched as though contemplating an implacable
deity at a Himalayan distance. Jesus adopted the posture of a
child kneeling at a parent's thigh or lap: prayer should be silent,
secret, private. The way in which a prayer was said was characteristic of Jesus's teaching, which was to reverse all the as-
sumptions. He turned the world, which was wrong and false,
upside down and set it upright. When he taught his disciples,
and the people as a whole, how to behave, there was a stunning
reversal of values, which must have caused astonishment. He
produced a series of precepts, known as the Beatitudes, which
are part of the Sermon on the Mount in Matthew 5:3–12 and
the Sermon on the Plain in Luke 6:20–23. These should be
taken in conjunction with other admonitions of Jesus's scattered through the Gospels, which he taught as a guide through
life and its material problems. The world was reversed, and
poverty and humility were substituted for pride, ambitions, hierarchies, and pursuit of power, money, and pleasure.

We must bear in mind that the land where Jesus preached
was a place of contrasts, often savage ones. The long and economically successful reign of Herod the Great had produced
prosperity for many, and great wealth for a few. The end of
piracy, the expansion of trade, and the stability of the new
Roman Empire had made it possible for traders to make rapid

fortunes and careful farmers to do well year after year. But as Jesus said, "The poor always ye have with you" (Jn 12:8), and prosperity had attracted countless immigrants from the north and east who formed pockets of poverty everywhere. The Jews looked after their own poor—they were more conscientious in this respect than any other people—but beggars, cripples, lepers, the demented, and the confused were ubiquitous. Moreover, charity itself was a source of pride. Jesus always stressed not the action, however virtuous in appearance, but the feeling behind it. He saw that the successful man turned philanthropist could be a monster of arrogance, just as poverty bred meanness, violence, and cruelty. What he looked for was the "poor in spirit," a new term he added to the human language, meaning someone whose thoughts were above material things and whose mind simply did not calculate in terms of possessions.

Hence "Blessed are the poor in spirit: for theirs is the kingdom of heaven" is the first of the Beatitudes Jesus lists in the fifth chapter of Matthew. Those who sorrow will be comforted, the meek will inherit the earth, those who hunger and thirst after justice will be filled, the merciful will be shown pity, the pure in heart will see the beatific vision, the peacemakers will be treated as God's children, and those who are persecuted because they do right will go straight to God. Luke repeats the gist of this teaching but adds a series of warnings aimed at those who are ambitious to do well in the world (6:24–26).

Many of them will prosper, but only in this world, not the next. "[W]oe unto you that are rich! for ye have received your consolation. Woe unto you that are full! for ye shall hunger. Woe unto you that laugh now! for ye shall mourn and weep." Jesus said they should be particularly worried "when all men shall speak well of you!" It meant there was something fundamentally false about what they were doing, or saying, or thinking.

This was tough teaching, hard to follow, and entirely new. It had no equivalent in the Old Testament or any of the pious wisdom literature of the ancient Near East. And Jesus, according to Luke, followed it with still more difficult maxims (6:27–29): "Love your enemies, do good to them which hate you, Bless them that curse you, and pray for them which despitefully use you. And unto him that smiteth thee on the one cheek offer also the other; and him that taketh away thy cloke forbid not to take thy coat also." Above all, he told them, hesitate to criticize other people: "Judge not, and ye shall not be judged: condemn not, and ye shall not be condemned; forgive, and ye shall be forgiven" (6:37).

In all this teaching, Jesus was stressing that it was not so much the outer actions but the inner sentiments which mattered. In an important passage in Matthew (5:21–48; 6:1–34), Jesus stressed that evil feelings allowed to develop unrestrained led to major sins. It had always been obvious that killing was wrong, he argued. "But I say unto you, That whosoever is angry with his brother without a cause" was sinful, too. It was wrong to abuse or swear at another man, and "whosoever shall say, Thou fool, shall be in danger of hell fire." So compose quarrels, "be reconciled to thy brother," and "[a]gree with thine adversary quickly, whilst thou art in the way with him." Of course, adultery was wrong—everyone knew that—"But I say unto you, That whosoever looketh on a woman to lust after her hath committed adultery with her already in his heart." Swearing was wrong, and he gave examples to avoid. Speech should be simple and direct: "[L]et your communication be, Yea, yea; Nay, nay: for whatsoever is more than these cometh of evil." The old saying "Thou shalt love thy neighbour, and hate thine enemy" was wrong: "I say unto you, Love your enemies, bless them that curse you, do good to them that hate you, and pray for them which despitefully use you, and persecute you." He begged his listeners to do these things "[t]hat ye may be the children of your Father which is in heaven: for he maketh his sun to rise on the evil and the good, and sendeth rain on the just and on the unjust." He continued, "Be ye therefore perfect, even as your Father which is in heaven is perfect." Alms should be given secretly, not publicly: "[L]et not thy left hand know what thy right hand doeth." Do not make a parade of praying in the street, but "enter into thy closet, and when thou has shut the door pray to thy Father." When fasting, don't go about with a woeful face but carry on normally—make sacrifices, like prayers, secret.

The transience and pointlessness of the world, when contrasted with the solidity and the permanence of heaven, was a theme to which he turned repeatedly. "Lay not up for yourselves treasures upon earth, where moth and rust doth corrupt, and where thieves break through and steal: But lay up for yourselves treasures in heaven. . . . For where your treasure is, there will your heart be also." Don't fuss about food or drink or clothes: "Is not the life more than meat, and the body than raiment?" The Father knows what you need, and he will provide. "[S]eek ye first the kingdom of God, and his righteousness; and all these things shall be added unto you. Take therefore no thought for the morrow. . . . Sufficient unto the day is the evil thereof."

Many of Jesus's sayings, thus recorded in Matthew and Luke, have become maxims familiar to us from childhood. But they were startlingly new in his day. They provoked thought, astonishment, often anger, fear, and doubt—and excitement. When Jesus preached in the fields, he set men and women arguing and thinking. Mark tells us that when Jesus was asked what was the Great Commandment, he cited the book of Deuteronomy: "thou shalt love the Lord thy God with all thy heart, and with all thy soul, and with all thy mind, and with all thy strength." He added an injunction from Leviticus: "Thou shalt love thy neighbour as thyself." It was Jesus who first drew these two Old Testament commands together, making them the center of the good life—"There is none other commandment greater than these." The scribe who had asked him the question noticed the innovation and commented in admiration that Jesus's answer "is more than all whole burnt offerings and sacrifices." To which Jesus replied, "Thou art not far from the Kingdom of God" (12:28-34). For not all scribes were blind and foolish, and Jesus could always recognize the decent ones.

When Jesus was asked "[W]ho is my neighbour?" (Lk 10:29), his answer was: everyone. He turned compassion, which all of us feel from time to time for a particular person, into a huge, overarching gospel of love. He taught the love of mankind as a whole. The Greek word for this is *philanthrōpia*, "philanthropy," which has since become threadbare with use and stained by misuse. It did not exist in Jesus's day as a concept. The idea of loving all humanity did not occur to anyone, Greek or barbarian, Jew or Gentile. Everyone's compassion—love—was selective. The Greeks were taught to hate the barbarians, just as Jews were taught to hate Gentiles and Samaritans. The Romans despised the peoples they conquered. All free men and women hated and feared slaves. Aristotle, perhaps the most sophisticated and enlightened man of his age, dismissed slaves as mere "animated machines." The intellectual, social, and racial climate of Jesus's day was implacably hostile to his message in this respect. The society he entered was one in which pious Jews taught and were taught that Gentiles without the law were accursed. What he tried to show was that compassion had, quite literally, no limits. Otherwise it was false. Benevolence was meaningless if it failed to be universal. Here was a new commandment as important as any in the Decalogue, or all of them together. God was the model. He loved *all* human beings. And anyone who drew distinctions and made exceptions on grounds of nationality or race or religious beliefs or opinions or age or sex or profession or past record of sinfulness was not heading for the Kingdom of God. On the contrary, he would find its gates shut.

One principal reason Christianity later spread all over the world was that Jesus himself was a universalist. "I . . . will draw all men unto me," he said in John 12:32. He insisted, "God so loved the world . . . that whosoever believeth in him should not perish, but have eternal life." God had sent him to earth not to condemn the world, or any part of it, "but that the world through him might be saved" (Jn 3:16–17). There are no restrictions or qualifications in this universal mission. When he gave his apostles their final instructions about their missionary tasks ahead, he set no geographical, social, national, or racial limits. They were to "go . . . into all the world" and "teach all nations" (Mk 16:15; Mt 28:19).

This universalism of Jesus stretched from his Incarnation to the Crucifixion. His mother was Jewish by birth but his Father was God, soaring above all personal distinctions. He had no home, no country, no race, no characteristics tying him to a tribe or a nation or a locality. He belonged to the Kingdom, outside time and space. But he was united to all men by love. He was philanthropy—the love of man—incarnate, and his sacrifice on the cross was the supreme philanthropic act in his life on earth and for all time: "Greater love hath no man than this, that a man lay down his life for his friends" (Jn 15:13). But by friends he meant all without exception. There was nothing exclusive about Jesus and his teaching. His message was the most inclusive of all such communications. No one before had, and no one since has, so confidently and warmly and indeed naturally opened his arms to the entire human race.

V

✝ Poetry and Parables,
Questions and Silence

THE APPEAL OF JESUS'S teaching is clear enough. For wherever he went, for the best part of three years, he attracted large crowds. It was not that his message was popular, though much of it was. But some of it made hard demands and set a high standard of virtue and self-sacrifice. Yet his teaching was mesmeric. All could hear it, though he often spoke to multitudes in the open. So his voice was distinct, and resonant. It pleased them all: there was no weariness. The truth is, Jesus was not so much a rhetorician, or a preacher, as a poet. He thought and reasoned and spoke as a poet does—in images, flashes of insight and metaphors from the world of nature. All the time he taught he was creating little pictures in the minds of the men and women who listened to him. He was the poet of virtue, the bard of righteousness, the minstrel of divine love.

His talk was a rhapsody and when he exhorted, his words formed palinodes and lyrics.

It is fitting that his birth should have been cast amid the three poems Luke reproduces in his Gospel. They are the Magnificat, or song of worship, spontaneously produced by his mother (1:46–55); the Benedictus, or blessing song of her cousin Elizabeth (1:68–79); and the Nunc Dimittis, or spiritual farewell of Simeon, an old Temple servant (2:29–32). All have been set to music many times and are spoken in civilized tongues. Jesus's poetry was the poetry of speech rather than rhyme. Sometimes, indeed, it was rhythmic. Thus the Beatitudes as given in Matthew 5:3–12 are marked by what students of verse call synthetic parallelism, in which the second line of each verse completes the meaning of the first line. And in Matthew 11:28–30 there are strong rhythms in Jesus's beautiful hymn to labor, which I have taken the liberty of setting in verse:

> Come unto me, all ye that labour
> > and are heavy laden,
> and I will give you rest.
> Take my yoke upon you,
> > and learn of me;
> for I am meek and lowly in heart:
> and ye shall find rest unto your souls.
> For my yoke is easy,
> and my burden is light.

Jesus's words sometimes straddle the border between prose and poetry, as in this passage (Mt 8:20):

> The foxes have holes,
> and the birds of the air have nests;
> but the Son of man hath not where
> to lay his head.

In John 21:18 there is a passage about the old:

> When thou wast young,
> thou girdedst thyself,
> and walkedst whither thou wouldest:
> but when thou shalt be old,
> thou shalt stretch forth thy hands,
> and another shall gird thee,
> and carry thee whither thou wouldest not.

Even when rhythm is lacking and the form is prosaic, Jesus's words are never far from the poetic, for they are rich in metaphor and simile, in vivid comparisons with the world of nature. There are not half a dozen lines of his teaching without an image, and often an unforgettable one, which has entered into the repertoire of writers all over the world. Inanimate objects spring to life, animals are anthropomorphized, nature teems with purposeful moral activity, and human beings often assume a

dignity, a profundity, or a pathos, thanks to the brilliant glitter
of Jesus's imagery. We hear of "living water" (Jn 4:10) and "the
blind lead[ing] the blind" (Lk 6:39). Jesus wishes to gather the
children of Jerusalem together "as a hen doth gather her brood
under her wings" (Lk 13:34). There is a wonderful image of the
simple farmer who should sow "night and day" and "the seed
should spring and grow up, he knoweth not how" (Mk 4:27).
Jesus loves single trees, standing in isolation, the olive, the fig,
the vine, and uses them tenderly. He speaks of the late summer
and the whitening harvests. He loves roots, branches, and leaves,
and sees images of people in all of them. When he uses words
to conjure up a picture, it is striking how often the phrases he
creates have become part of the furniture of literature: "The
wind bloweth where it listeth, and thou hearest the sound
thereof, but canst not tell whence it cometh, and whither it
goeth" (Jn 3:8). And in Matthew 11:7 he asks, "What went ye
out into the wilderness to see? A reed shaken with the wind?"
When Jesus says, "[L]et the dead bury their dead" (Mt 8:22),
he brings us up short, startled. "I came not to send peace, but
a sword," he says in Matthew 10:34, and startles us again. He
is fond of fire images: "I am come to send fire on the earth; and
what will I, if it be already kindled?" (Lk 12:49). "Every sacrifice," he says in Mark 9:49, "shall be salted with fire." Salt
images are another favorite: "Salt is good: but if the salt have
lost his savour, wherewith shall it be seasoned?" (Lk 14:34). He

tells his disciples, "Ye are the salt of the earth" (Mt 5:13). And we hear of salt cast on the dunghill. Time and again he tells us of the beauties of nature, of God "cloth[ing] the grass of the field" (Mt 6:30), of lilies so dressed by the deity that "Solomon in all his glory was not arrayed like one of these" (Mt 6:29; Lk 12:27). There is a fascinating passage in Luke in which a gardener shows pity for his fig tree and begs the owner not to cut it down when it bears no fruit for three years: "Lord, let it alone this year also, till I shall dig about it, and dung it: And if it bear fruit, well: and if not, then after that thou shalt cut it down" (13:7–9).

Jesus loves the figure or metaphor of the cup which God handed him, and which he must drink: he uses it three times (Mt 20:22; Lk 22:20, 42; Jn 18:11). As I have already noted, he speaks of sheep and shepherds constantly—more often than any other rustic image—the safe folding of the sheep, the guarding of the sheep from wolves, the differences between the true shepherd and the hireling, the fact that the shepherd knows his sheep and that they recognize him and his voice, the way in which sheep become scattered and some lost, and the fidelity of the shepherd who leaves his flock to seek the stray and rejoices mightily when he finds it. "I am the good shepherd," says Jesus, "and know my sheep, and am known of mine" (Jn 10:14; Mt 18:12, 9:36, 26:31; Lk 15:4). He also says, "I am the light of the world" (Jn 9:5). Light and its contrast with darkness is Jesus's favorite image of all, which he uses with great power and passion. He comes, he says, to "work the works of him that sent me, while it is day: for the night cometh, when no man can work" (Jn 9:4). The whole of John, from the Gospel's stunning first paragraphs, is an epic prose poem to light. In these paragraphs, the word "light" is compared to the knowledge of God's truth, "the true Light, which lighteth every man that cometh into the world" (1:9). Throughout the ministry of Jesus there are striking contrasts between the light of truth and the darkness of ignorance, Satan, and evil. Jesus was always eager to make the blind see because such an act illustrated and epitomized his mission—"seeing" was "knowing," recognizing truth and following it.

The Gospel of John also makes clear that in Jesus's teaching there is a continuum between the word, the light, and the life. Jesus came into the world to speak the word: "He that heareth my word . . . is passed from death into life" (5:24). Jesus always emphasized that the physical death of which we speak is only "falling asleep." The true death is sin. By contrast, "life" is the future Kingdom, outside time and everlasting. In the prologue of John, a vast metaphor of light is the key phrase: "In him was life; and the life was the light of men" (1:4). This is a poetic image, but it is also a philosophical one. It is Jesus's position, as a moralist, that human beings, despite sin and all their frailties, have a natural inclination to truth. It is revealed by the word, the Logos; that is, Jesus: This word of truth attracts God's children to the light as a magnet attracts metals while mere stones are unmoved. To love the light is to love the truth. It is a profoundly philosophical point but one, curiously enough, which simple, uneducated people grasp instinctively because it is also a poetic one.

Light and darkness: the Gospels are the verbal stages upon which Jesus's message is enacted in the strongest chiaroscuro, gradual dawnings breaking into floods of intense light, gathering clouds piling up thunderously, lit by lightning flashes and then dispersed—a darkness truly satanic which finally yields to a light so intense and all-penetrating as to be truly heavenly. Darkness and light are constantly stressed in Jesus's mission, and then, in real, tragic life, culminate in the twilight Last Supper, the dusk in the Garden Agony of Gethsemane, the darkness of the Crucifixion, and finally the dawn of the third day revealing the blinding light of the Resurrection. Seen thus in the living metaphor, the life of Jesus is the incarnation of light, its growth, spread, and reception, its extinction, and its miraculous rekindling into an everlasting incandescence.

That is the poetry of Jesus's teaching. But he was also a storyteller, and the particular form of storytelling he favored was the parable. Parables are so important in the New Testament and he is so closely associated with this art form that he is often credited with inventing it. In fact, parables occur in other texts of the ancient Near East, and there are several in the Old Testament. The rabbis who came before and after Jesus used them. But their object was to explain difficult texts: they were a device of that dreary and eternal science called "commentary." The essence of a Jesus parable is to stimulate thought, to encourage people to think for themselves, to puzzle out religious mysteries—a mystery is a secret revealed by God that would not have been known had he not revealed it. A parable helps to alleviate the problem of expressing supernatural things in natural language. Jesus sometimes indicated why he used parables. Mark suggests that Jesus drew a distinction between his spiritually educated disciples and his general congregation (4:11ff.): "But without a parable spake he not unto them: and when they were alone, he expounded all things to his disciples." When addressing his elect, he said, "Unto you it is given to know the mystery of the kingdom of God: but unto them that are without, all these things are done in parables." This episode, in which knowledge is treated as a possession, contains the difficult verse 25: "For he that hath, to him shall be given: and he that hath not, from him shall be taken even that which he hath." This seems unreasonable, as well as unjust, if seen in terms of material goods. But Jesus speaks of understanding. Those who develop skills in grasping will get more, but those without understanding have to be deprived of their false knowledge in order to start again.

The point is that Jesus's teaching, what we call Christianity, is both a much more simple religion than the Judaism Jesus was superseding—Judaism has endless observances, each nested in a cocoon of commentaries—and a more complex one, because it involves a change of heart. So its practice cannot be laid down by laws: it requires an inner impulse. Jesus was always aware of this difficult dimension of his teaching, and the parables were designed to set the inner impulse in motion. They are indeed highly emotional, and are intended to be. Jesus was entirely rational but also a very emotional person who evoked and responded to emotions in others. The parable was his particular method of arousing and directing emotions.

The Gospel of John does not speak of parables, though it has some: the vine in chapter 15 and the Good Shepherd in chapter 10. There are four parables in Mark, but the rest are short comparisons. Most of the parables appear in Matthew and Luke. Matthew has eight parables about the Kingdom of God/Heaven in chapter 13, plus others in chapter 18 (the lost sheep and the unmerciful servant), chapter 20 (the workers in the vineyard), chapter 21 (the two sons and the wicked tenants), chapter 22 (the great banquet), and chapter 25 (the ten virgins and the talents). Luke has the most parables; they are bunched up in chapters 10 to 20 and grouped together according to subject matter: trust, anxiety, and final reckoning; feasts;

losing things; use and abuse of wealth; and prayer. It is difficult to give an exact total: sixty to sixty-five according to one definition, but another, stricter reckoning reduces the figure to forty. Matthew and Luke often give slightly different versions of the same parable. Seven parables appear in all three synoptics: the new cloth in the old coat, the new wine in the old wineskin, the sower and the different soils, the lamp under the bushel, the mustard seed, the fig tree, and the tenants. These are not necessarily the most important ones. Indeed, the two masterpieces of the parable form, the Good Samaritan and the prodigal son, occur only in Luke (10:30–37, 15:11–32), as does another striking story, Lazarus the beggar and the wicked rich man (16:19–31). The workers in the vineyard parable is found in Matthew alone, as is the sinister tale of the unmerciful servant and the beautiful fantasy of the ten virgins.

It was a convention of the parable that it be told as a true tale (no matter how improbable) and that the listeners accept it as a factual one. This is particularly important in the case of the Good Samaritan. That the traveler "fell among thieves" on the Jericho road who robbed, battered, and stripped him was only too likely: the route east from Jerusalem was notorious for such crimes, as indeed it still was when I first traveled it over half a century ago. Equally likely was that the priests and Levites "passed by on the other side." Jesus's audience was happy to believe the clerical class as a whole to be hypocritical and uncharitable. But the compassion and generosity of the Samaritan merchant—who not only tended the distressed man but arranged for him to be looked after at the inn and his accommodations paid for until he was fit—has to be credible. The Samaritans were hated by the Jews—not least the people of Galilee, who were separated from Judaea by Samaria—with a passion which was irrational and hard for us to understand. It was a quasi-religious fury and a form of local racism of the most ferocious temper. Jesus told this tale in response to the query "[W]ho is my neighbour?" He told it so well and so convincingly that the Good Samaritan has gone down in history and literature, in art and drama, as the ideal neighbor to a man in distress. Jesus was illustrating the universalist principle which was perhaps the most important element in his social message: we are all neighbors, one to another, and our human fellowship depends on kindness and charity, not tribe or race or color or nationality. The tale was meant to shock a Jewish audience into recognizing this truth, and shock them it did, because its artful verisimilitude made them believe it. It is an ennobling story nobly told: for more than two millennia, people in countries all over the world, for whom the term has no meaning except in the parable, have sought to be "the Good Samaritan."

The tale has a secondary meaning: like twelve other parables, it deals with the money factor. First-century Palestine had a money economy; we hear nothing of barter. Moreover, since Jerusalem was a place of annual pilgrimage for the enormous number of Jews living within the Roman Empire, many different coins of copper, alloy, silver, even gold were in circulation. The money changers of the Temple were needed to enable pilgrims to buy the doves and lambs for their sacrifices—Jesus's complaint was that they encroached on Temple precincts. Jesus had a robust attitude toward money, commerce, and wealth. All his sympathies lay with the poor, as many parables testify. He never made the mistake of supposing that poverty made people virtuous. But he was painfully aware that wealth offered endless opportunities for corruption. The parable of Lazarus the beggar and the wicked rich man, so vividly recounted in Luke 16:19–31, shows how wealth can dominate the life of a thoughtless and self-indulgent person who "was clothed in purple and fine linen, and fared sumptuously every day." By contrast Lazarus, who was sick—"the dogs came and licked his sores"—lay at the rich man's gate to get the crumbs which fell from his table. Jesus taught that "there is a great gulf fixed" between rich and poor in this life, and that the rich who do nothing about it will discover the gulf exists in the next world, where the poor will be "comforted" and the rich "tormented." Luke 15:8–9 tells the story of the woman who had ten pieces of silver, lost one, lit a candle, and swept the house diligently until she found it, then called her friends and neigh-

bors together and said, "Rejoice with me." Jesus does not re-
proach her for being miserly or avaricious—he implies she was
poor and the lost coin was a serious matter—but uses the story
to make the lost coin stand for the "joy in the presence of the
angels of God over one sinner that repenteth." Jesus's general
point about wealth is that it all depends on what you do with
it. As the philosopher of universal philanthropy, the process
whereby the instinct of compassion is made generally useful
among mankind, Jesus was eager to encourage all who had
wealth to distribute a generous portion of it to the poor. He did
not foolishly suppose that in his life poverty could be eradi-
cated by reforms, let alone charity (indeed, he admitted that
"the poor always ye have with you" when encouraging a woman
to anoint him with precious ointment). But he insisted it was
right for all to exercise charity, even if their means were slen-
der: one of the most touching images in the entire New Testament is of the poor widow who insisted on contributing to the
Temple charity box her "two mites, which make a farthing"
(Mk 12:42). This was all she had to spend each day.

In telling the parable of the Good Samaritan, Jesus describes a case where money promotes virtue. This merchant
was industrious and provident. He did a good trade and used
its proceeds to help others as well as his own family. A less
successful man might also have felt compassion for the battered
traveler but could have done little about it. The Samaritan had

earned and saved the means to enable the poor man to make a complete recovery, and he used them for this purpose. Here was money honestly made and judiciously spent.

Many of the parables deal with the theme of lost and found, a favorite image of Jesus's; he used it as a variant on his light-and-darkness metaphors. Just after Luke presents the story of the woman who found her lost silver coin, he adds the prodigal son tale, the most luminous, perhaps, of all the stories Jesus told. It raises many issues, which is one reason why it has attracted more comment, and has been the subject of more illustrations by artists, than any other parable. The younger son of a wealthy man demands his portion, receives it, then wastes it on "riotous living" in a "far country." A famine comes and he falls into want. He becomes a swineherd, "and he would fain have filled his belly with the husks that the swine did eat." He repents, concludes he has sinned against God and his father, and decides to return home in humility and say to his father, "[I] am no more worthy to be called thy son: make me as one of thy hired servants." Instead, when his father sees him "when he was yet a great way off," he receives his son with open arms and kills the fatted calf for a feast of thanksgiving. The well-behaved elder son protests in the name of justice. But his father tells him, "[T]hou art ever with me, and all that I have is thine. It was meet that we should make merry, and be glad: for this thy brother was dead, and is alive again; and was lost, and is found."

The primary point of the parable, then, is the repentance of the sinner and the joy this brings to the righteous. Jesus often stresses that the return of the penitent brings more rejoicing in heaven than the goodness of many worthy persons. This is unjust, perhaps—and certainly the elder son thought so. But heaven is not so much about justice but mercy. In strict justice no one would be saved, but thanks to the infinite mercy of God, even the worst sinners have a chance provided they admit their wrongdoing and strive to lead a different life. The story is so vivid, however, and the three men concerned emerge so clearly in a few brilliant strokes of narrative, that endless comment is provoked. Is not the father foolish, or at least thoughtless? Foolish in giving his pleasure-loving son his portion in the first place: inevitably he would waste it. Thoughtless in not letting his good elder son, who is out working hard in the fields, know that his prodigal brother has returned and that a feast is being prepared. Instead he goes ahead, and the first the good son knows of it is when he comes from work, tired and sweaty, and hears the sound of "musick and dancing." No wonder he is "angry, and would not go in." One suspects that the prodigal has always been the father's favorite—and one wonders what will happen in the sequel. Will foolishness start again? Will the good son, in exasperation, finally demand his portion and set up his own farm? One wonders about the mother, too, and her absence. Dead? Marginalized into insignificance? Or were there two mothers? The surmises aroused by the story are endless: a sure sign it is a good one.

But many parables raise unanswered questions. Jesus loved conviviality, and though he might condemn the rich man for faring sumptuously every night—knowing there was a hungry man at his door—he never condemned generous hospitality. Many of his most telling lessons were taught around crowded tables, and he often used feasts to make his points. Chapter 14 of Luke is about two of them. The first he uses to stress his point that presumption is punished and modesty rewarded—if you take an unwarrantably high place at a feast you will be put down, whereas if you abase yourself you may be told, "Friend, go up higher": "For whosoever exalteth himself shall be abased; and he that humbleth himself shall be exalted" (14:10–11).

That is straightforward. But what do we make of the parable that immediately follows (14:6–24): "A certain man made a great supper, and bade many"? But his guests made excuses: the "certain man" was not as popular as he thought. So, as the food had been bought, he sent his servant out "into the streets and lanes of the city" and invited in "the poor, and the maimed, and the halt, and the blind." And when this still left a place empty, he told his servant to scour "the highways and hedges, and compel them to come in, that [his] house may be filled." The feast is plainly an image of the Kingdom of Heaven, but the details baffle interpretation. Indeed, St. Augustine used the phrase "compel them to come in" to justify forcible conversion of heretics. The angry lord says, "[N]one of those men which were bidden shall taste of my supper." But why should he suppose they had changed their minds and now wished to come? Was it because they resented the poor taking their original places? One sometimes feels that part of the parable has been omitted. Thus, the story of the unmerciful servant whose debts are forgiven by the king, but who then has an underling cast into prison for comparable debts, illustrates the principle of "Do as you would be done by." But as Matthew tells it (18:23–35), it is crude, and the king's anger in having the unjust servant handed over to the tormentors is unmerciful. In the parable of the vineyard tenants in Luke 20:9–20, their behavior is so outrageous to the owner—first beating his servants, then killing his son and heir—that verisimilitude is lost, and interest correspondingly wanes. The lord destroys the husbandmen and gives the vineyard to others. The moral is the same as in the great banquet, and Jesus tells his audience: "The stone which the builders rejected, the same is become the head of the corner? Whosoever shall fall upon that stone shall be broken; but on whomsoever it shall fall, it will grind him to powder." Luke says that "the chief priests and the scribes" believed Jesus had "spoken this parable against them," and "the same hour sought to lay hands on him." Hence we conclude that the parable was not of general application but was specifically aimed at a particular group of wicked people.

But what are we to say of the unjust steward in Luke 16:1–8? Facing the sack for wasting his lord's goods, he uses his lord's substance to curry favor among his debtors so that "when [he is] put out of [his] stewardship, they may receive [him] into their houses." He has no other way to live: "I cannot dig; to beg I am ashamed." The lord commends the unjust steward "because he had done wisely: for the children of this world are in their generation wiser than the children of light." Jesus's subsequent explanation of the moral mechanics of the parable—at least as recorded by Luke, who may have muddled it or omitted a vital detail—is unenlightening, though his final moral is perfectly clear and sensible: "No servant can serve two masters: for either he will hate the one, and love the other, or else he will hold to the one and despise the other. Ye cannot serve God and mammon" (16:13). Jesus appears to be condemning avarice, for in verse 14, Luke adds: "And the Pharisees also, who were covetous, heard all these things: and they derided him." Jesus then drew a sharp distinction between "they which justify yourselves before men" and God who "knoweth your hearts." Jesus concludes resoundingly: "[T]hat which is highly esteemed among men is abomination in the sight of God" (16:15).

Here is a case where the moral is excellent, but the story leading up to it is mysterious. The story of the five foolish and five wise virgins and their oil lamps is vivid and delightful

(Mt 25:1–13). But the wise virgins are mean and do not share their oil with the foolish ones; and the tardy bridegroom is unjust to shut the foolish girls out. Yet the moral is pertinent: "Watch therefore, for ye know neither the day nor the hour wherein the Son of man cometh." The parable of the talents which immediately follows (Mt 25:14–40) is akin to the story of the unjust steward in Luke. It takes as a fact of life the economics of worldliness, commends lending at high interest, and cites the wisdom of a lord who reaps "where [he] hast not sown" and gathers "where [he] hast not strawed." It includes the notorious verse 29: "For unto every one that hath shall be given, and he shall have abundance: but from him that hath not shall be taken away even that which he hath." Unlike in Mark 4:25, in this instance Jesus is not speaking of knowledge but of property. Jesus adds: "[C]ast ye the unprofitable servant into outer darkness: for there shall be weeping and gnashing of teeth."

That, we take it, is the wisdom of the world. For Jesus immediately passes to the judgment where the unworldly are divided from the worldly: "And he shall set the sheep on his right hand, but the goats on the left" (Mt 25:33). He tells the sheep: "Come, ye blessed of my Father, inherit the kingdom prepared for you" (25:34). Jesus goes on to explain that those in this world who feed the hungry and the thirsty, and who take in homeless strangers, and who clothe the naked, and who visit the sick and the imprisoned shall be rewarded, and he makes the striking point that whoever befriends "the least of these my brethren, ye have done it unto me" (25:40).

The parables, taken as a whole, are a vast dichotomy of contrasts expressed in stories and images. Darkness and light, this world and the next, outward show and inner goodness, sheep and goats, material wisdom and spiritual simplicity, rich in goods and poor in spirit, cunning and innocence. There is every sign that when Jesus told his stories the people listening clamored for more. So the parables should be seen both in groups and in their totality for their meanings to be made plain and consistent. Jesus was sometimes subtle and mysterious and even obscure in detail, but his distinction between right and wrong always emerged before he had finished. He left his hearers to talk and argue among themselves. That was his intention. His gift was not only to teach but to encourage people to teach one another, to take seriously the question of what constitutes the good life and to debate it earnestly.

This brings us to two characteristics of Jesus which emerge strongly from the language of the Gospels. The first was his habit of asking questions. He may have acquired this from study of the sacred texts. The Old Testament abounds in questions. God often asks questions, usually awkward ones. The question is part of the artistic form of the book of Job, and is used by Yahweh to convey vast amounts of information and to delineate his power. In chapter 38 of Job alone the Lord asks fifty-eight questions, from "who is this that darkeneth counsel by word without knowledge?" (38:2) to "Where wast thou when I laid the foundations of the earth?" (38:4). To ask questions was also part of Jesus's method of teaching. He spoke with great authority and had a great deal to impart, but he was anxious, if possible, to extract the knowledge and thoughts of his auditors, especially his disciples. "Whom do men say that I am?" (Mk 8:27) is a characteristic Jesus question. Mark shows him asking questions constantly. Thus before the feeding of the five thousand he asks, "How many loaves have ye?" (6:38). On the same occasion, John has Jesus ask Philip, "Whence shall we buy bread, that these may eat?" (6:5). Jesus was an inclusive teacher, indeed an inclusive person generally, who constantly sought to draw all those present into the discussion, the elucidation of truth, the perception of reality. In Mark he introduces the parable of the mustard seed by a sharp double question: "Whereunto shall we liken the kingdom of God? or with what comparison shall we compare it?" (4:30). When, at the beginning of his ministry, just after his baptism, he sees Andrew and another following him, he asks, "What seek ye?" (Jn 1:38). His questions to his intimates are often profound, poignant, even pleading. When many find his doctrine on the bread of life too difficult—"This is an hard saying; who can hear it?"—and leave, Jesus asks, "Doth this offend you?

What and if ye shall see the Son of man ascend up where he was before?" When "many of his disciples went back, and walked no more with him," Jesus said to the Twelve, "Will ye also go away?" (Jn 6:60–67). (Immediately afterward, referring to Judas Iscariot, he asks, "Have not I chosen you twelve, and one of you is a devil?" [6:71].) He even asks such questions as "Have I been so long time with you, and yet hast thou not known me?" (Jn 14:9). And, finally, "Do you love me?" After the Resurrection, he asks Mary Magdalene, "Woman, why weepst thou? Whom seekest thou?" (Jn 20:15). What all these questions—and there are many others recorded—have in common is that Jesus knows the answers even before he asks them. Their function is to extend a hand in welcome, in interest, in affection. They are a form of embrace, even when they are critical.

Equally characteristic, though used for a variety of purposes, are Jesus's silences. Though a teacher, an exponent, a man whose primary duty in life he regarded as discoursing, Jesus made highly effective use of both the question and the silence to get across his message. His questions, as often as not, were statements and conveyed information. Equally his silences were a form of mute speech. And often they carried a weight which words could not. There is a passage in Thomas Carlyle's *Sartor Resartus* which has a particular application to Jesus's ministry: "Speech is of time, silence is of eternity. Thought will not work except in silence. Neither will virtue work except in secrecy." Up to the age of thirty, Jesus was silent, or at least unrecorded—and there is no indication he wished it otherwise. He was silent, virtually, during his temptations, until the end. He was silent during his baptism. He was silent when he changed the water into wine at Cana. Indeed, he was habitually silent during his miracles, except in bidding the lame to walk or the dead to arise. And he enjoined silence about them. He was habitually silent about his powers, except when necessary, and about his divinity, as it was important to establish the nature of his character as a man. When told "Thou art the Christ, the Son of the living God" (Mt 16:16), he enjoins silence again. He was usually silent to direct questions. He preferred to answer the thought rather than the words. He expresses the silence of shame when presented with the woman taken in adultery: shame not at her sin but at the sins of those who wished to stone her to death. He prefers to write their shame in the dust rather than speak it. In the whole incident, one of the most vivid and moving in the entire New Testament, he uses only two sentences: "Woman, where are those thine accusers? hath no man condemned thee?" and "Neither do I condemn thee; go, and sin no more" (Jn 8:10–11). He is silent on horrors: at the death of John the Baptist, for instance. He is silent, with indignation, before Caiaphas. He shows the silence of contempt before Herod Antipas. In his physical sufferings he is silent with self-absorption and pity for his assailants and mockers.

His silence on the cross was as striking as his rare words, the seven last sayings.

Jesus the teacher is eloquent but succinct. It is uncommon to find him using two words when one will do. The thoughts, and their intensity, conveyed in his instruction and parables are remarkable for their economy of words. Yet they give no impression of abruptness or brevity. The manner is invariably relaxed. The detail is always there when required. But the silences are an essential part of the ministry, too. His speech was silver, but we weigh his silences in gold.

VI

✝ Encounters: Men, Women,
Children, the Aged

ALTHOUGH JESUS constantly addressed crowds in synagogues, in the open, and in packed private houses, he spoke directly to each individual who composed them. It was his gift and also his philosophy. Each human being was a unique, priceless entity loved by God as a person, so that, as Jesus said, "the very hairs of your head are all numbered" (Lk 12:7). Jesus's love of people, as individuals, was in some way his most striking characteristic. He never tired of talking to them and penetrating their secrets. They were drawn to him and only too willing to divulge them. His life was a series of public meetings punctuated by casual encounters which turned into significant events. Jesus not only encouraged these encounters but treasured them. He remembered every word spoken. He clearly recounted them to his disciples, and that is how they reached the evangelists, who recorded them for us. For in most of them Jesus and the individual concerned were alone together—even if a babbling, pushing crowd surrounded them. These episodes, though often brief, form the human core of the New Testament and provide a unique satisfaction to the reader. There is nothing like them in the entire literature of the ancient world, sacred or secular.

Jesus's encounter with Andrew, immediately after his baptism, is a foretaste. It was Andrew who came up to him (with a companion who is nameless). There was something about Jesus's appearance, the way he held himself, the steadiness of his gaze, which attracted people. They felt he was open, that he would receive them as a friend and talk to them. Indeed, Jesus's manifest and responsive friendliness was his most striking quality, and it was apparent from the start. He directed it to all, but made each feel selected and treasured. Yet there was nothing professional about it. It came from his heart—there could be no mistake about that. According to John 1:37–42, when Andrew and his friend followed Jesus, he turned and said, "What seek ye?" Andrew said, "Master, where dwellest thou?" To which Jesus replied, "Come and see." They "abode with him that day: for it was about the tenth hour." The exact time when Andrew met Jesus is not obviously relevant, yet somehow it seems so. The friendship ripened immediately, and Andrew introduced his brother Simon to Jesus the next day.

There was an instant rapport, so that Jesus immediately gave Simon a new name, or nickname, Cephas (or Peter), meaning solid as the rock. He gave John and James, another pair of brothers, a nickname, too: "sons of thunder" (Mk 3:17). Jesus loved such names as a pledge of friendship or intimacy. Their use among themselves sealed their comradeship in their immense task of turning the world upside down, making spiritual values triumph over material ones. It is curious to think that this haphazard and unplanned meeting with Andrew was to begin a long story which was to end, for him and his brother, as well as for Jesus, with death on the cross: Simon Peter pinned upside down, at his request, so as not to compete with his divine master in the dignity of death; Andrew martyred at Patras in Achaea—bound, not nailed, so as to prolong the agony, on a cross whose peculiar shape has become the symbol of Scotland.

Jesus's summoning of Matthew from his busy tax collector's bench at the frontier with Syria is another striking encounter. This official, powerful but hated, followed immediately. It was an instant friendship, silent—no exchange of words is recorded—but strong, and it brought Jesus into the center of another world. For Matthew, clearly at Jesus's invitation, brought many of his colleagues and friends to an impromptu feast at the house where Jesus was staying. It was a huge success and attracted critical attention from the orthodox Jews and Pharisees, who asked the disciples, "Why eateth your Master with publicans and sinners?" (Mt 9:11). To which Jesus replied, "I will have mercy, and not sacrifice: for I am not come to call the righteous, but sinners to repentance."

This calling, followed by a feast, illustrated Jesus's habit, springing from his partly private, partly gregarious temperament, of mingling close encounters with communal ones. He loved to teach at mealtimes. So many of his images concerned bread and its breaking and distribution, as well as the cup and its drinking. The Last Supper was merely the awesome climax of these sacred convivialities. With the exception of spreading news of his miracles, Jesus was always open. He enjoyed food. The wine circulated. The talk flowed. But he respected the need of others for privacy, even secrecy. One of the most striking of his encounters was with Nicodemus, a Jew of high position, a Pharisee and a spiritual ruler who was prominent in the hierarchy (Jn 3:1–21). He "came to Jesus by night," so as not to jeopardize his position, and Jesus did not rebuke him for cowardice. On the contrary, he received him kindly and explained to him, in memorable words, much of his inner message. A man must be "born again" to see the Kingdom. Nicodemus asked, "How can a man be born when he is old? can he enter the second time into his mother's womb, and be born?" Jesus's answer was a plea for faith: "For God so loved the world, that he gave his only begotten Son, that whosoever believeth in him should not perish, but should have everlasting life." He told Nicodemus that he had not been sent "to condemn the world; but that the world through him might be saved." But, he hinted, he must sooner or later come into the open. He must not shun the light: "For every one that doeth evil hateth the light, neither cometh to the light, lest his deeds should be reproved." Nicodemus should "cometh to the light, that his deeds may be made manifest." This advice was eventually taken, for when Jesus's body was taken down from the cross, Nicodemus "brought a mixture of myrrh and aloes, about an hundred pounds weight." With this Jesus was anointed, and his body wound "in linen clothes with the spices" and buried in "a new sepulchre, wherein was never man yet laid." We assume that Nicodemus had prepared it for himself (Jn 19:39–42), though it may have belonged to Joseph of Arimathaea, who also assisted at the burial and had the stone rolled in front of the tomb. He, too, was a Jewish dignitary, a member of the Sanhedrin, or governing body of the community, who was a secret disciple.

Friendship with Nicodemus and Joseph illustrates the range of Jesus's circle, which included everyone who was drawn to him, irrespective of their social position or lack of it. A good example of his friendliness is the case of the royal official in Herod Antipas's service who comes to beg for the life of his little son (Jn 4:46–53). At first he beseeches Jesus to come in person, but then accepts that a mere word from Jesus will effect the miracle of healing. Jesus assures him that his faith is sufficient, and so it proves. This touching story is told by John with great tenderness, which reflects Jesus's own words spoken to the apostle and evangelist, for no one else heard the exchange. At the other end of the scale is the pathetic example of the elderly cripple who had haunted the pool of Bethesda for thirty-eight years (Jn 5:1–15). This medicinal pool, with its five flights of steps, or porches, into the waters, had an intermittent mineral spring, and when the waters "moved" (attributed to an angel) a cure was more likely, so there was competition to be the first in the flow after a "movement." The old man had no servants to drag him there quickly and so had had to watch, year after year, while others were cured and he remained "impotent," as John puts it. Jesus saw him there and seems to have known all about him, that he was a bit of a rogue, but was nevertheless moved to pity. He said, "Wilt thou be made whole?" The cripple said, "Sir, I have no man, when the water is troubled, to put me into the pool: but while I am coming, another steppeth down into the pool before me." Jesus said, "Rise, take up thy bed, and walk." The man was cured "immediately." Jesus later ran into him in the Temple and recognized him. He said, "Behold, thou art made whole: sin no more, lest a worse thing come unto thee." The man talked eagerly about his cure, as well he might, and that aroused the ire of the orthodox, for the miracle had occurred on the Sabbath. Some

interpret the passage as a sign of ingratitude: the former cripple betrayed Jesus by talking to the Jewish officials. But that
is surely wrong. The man had been unable to get about for
nearly forty years, and suddenly he was free and active. Naturally he went everywhere telling his tale to whoever would
listen.

There is a similar encounter in John 9:1–38 when Jesus
meets and cures a young man blind from birth. He was poor and
of no importance, and when he tried to tell people that a
marvelous thing had occurred, they bullied him. Was it not
the Sabbath when he was cured? How did it happen? Who did
it? Was not it a Sabbath-breaking sinner? The orthodox said,
"Give God the praise: we know that this man [Jesus] is a
sinner." At this point the young man exclaimed in exasperation, "Whether he be a sinner or no, I know not: one thing I
know, that, whereas I was blind, now I see." They argued with
him, bringing in Moses and whatnot, until he said, keeping in
the forefront the one thing that mattered to him—sight—that
restoring the sight of someone born blind had never been done
before in the history of the world: "If this man were not of God,
he could do nothing." They shouted at him, "Thou wast altogether born in sins, and dost thou teach us?" then "they cast
him out." When Jesus heard about this, he found the young
man and asked about his beliefs. The young man answered,
"Lord, I believe." And John concludes: "he worshipped him."

Here is another touching story of a brief encounter, with sight giving a perfect metaphor for knowledge of the truth.

Jesus's encounters with women had a particular significance. Women were almost invisible in the ancient Near East. They had little or no status unless they married rulers, and then their place was precarious. They might be discarded— "put away" was the term used in legal documents—at their husbands' whim. If they were poor and old, they were nothing. But not to Jesus. His keen eyes sought them out amid the multitude of figures who crowded round him. That is how he spotted the old widow putting her two mites into the collection box at the Temple. He commended her as an example of how even the poorest could possess generous hearts. Charity was not the easy prerogative of the rich but was a particular virtue of the needy and humble. We are left to speculate whether the widow, having given her daily coins, would have gone without food until the next morning. She and her mites thus pass into the literature of goodness just as surely as she passed into the Kingdom. Jesus could also sense goodness, even when he could not see it. Thus he became aware of the old woman who touched his garment believing her debilitating complaint would thus be cured. He felt her faith. Her spiritual need pulsed into him, and his power passed out and into her in response. So he identified that woman and praised her, and she knelt down and acknowledged his divinity. She was cured but, even more important, she passed into the spiritual repertoire of the humble believers, those whose faith in goodness towers over their insignificance.

But some of Jesus's encounters with women are more complicated than these simple instances. One of the most fascinating is his meeting at the well of Sychar, in Samaria, with a local woman who has come to draw water (Jn 4:4–42). The well had been dug by the patriarch Jacob and stood outside the town. Jesus and his disciples had to travel through Samaria every time they moved from Galilee to Judaea or vice versa. Jews were commanded to have no dealings with Samaritans, who were held to be accursed: though Hebrews by descent, they had their own shrine and religious customs. But that was exactly the kind of religious dogma Jesus held to be cruel and unreasonable. Being tired, he stopped at the well while his disciples went into the town to buy food. When he saw the woman he looked through her, and into her, as was his habit and his genius. He asked her for a drink of water from the well and got into conversation. She saw he was a Jew and thought it strange he was willing to talk to her. But she was happy to respond and was immediately fascinated by the distinction he drew between the water of the well, which soon left one thirsty again, and the spiritual water of truth, which was everlasting. She said, "Sir, give me this water, that I thirst not, neither come hither to draw." He said, perhaps smiling wryly to himself, for he knew all about her, "Go, call thy husband, and come hither." She replied, "I have no husband." This was what Jesus had been waiting for. He told her, "Thou hast well said, I have no husband: For thou hast had five husbands; and he whom thou now hast is not thy husband: in that saidst thou truly." The woman was astounded. But she was not a timid creature—Jesus had sensed this from the start—and had self-possession enough to respond, "Sir, I perceive that thou art a prophet." That gave Jesus the chance to explain to her that, however orthodox Jews and Samaritans might differ, they both had nothing in common with what he called "the true worshippers" who "shall worship the Father in spirit and in truth." For, he added, "God is a Spirit: and they that worship him must worship him in spirit and in truth." The question of rival shrines was irrelevant. The woman responded eagerly. She knew the Messiah was coming, she said, and "when he is come he will tell us all things." Jesus was beginning to explain—"I that speak unto thee am he"—when his disciples, arriving with the food they had bought, interrupted. They were very surprised indeed to find him talking to the woman, but they did not like to say so. Instead, they asked him to eat, but he declined: "I have meat to eat that ye know not of." He meant, of course, that his encounter with the woman had given him food for thought: how in doing "the will of him that sent me" (as he put it) he would include outsiders like the Samaritans who were eager to learn.

The woman, meanwhile, had left her pot and rushed back into the town, clamoring to all the men (we are told nothing about the women): "Come, see a man, which told me all things that ever I did: is not this the Christ?" The men, of course, came and were fascinated by Jesus; they persuaded him to spend two days with them and believed his message. The woman was pushed into the background: "Now we believe, not because of thy saying: for we have heard him ourselves." Perhaps she was notorious and unpopular among their wives. As with many other passages in the New Testament, we wish we had been told more. What was the explanation for her unusual marital arrangements, or lack of them? What more had Jesus told her about her life to explain her saying he "told me all things that ever I did"? It is strange that we know so much. For she did not talk to the evangelist John. Jesus must have given him the gist of his conversation with the woman, which John reproduces. And perhaps Jesus omitted much. As it is, she recedes into the darkness of history untold, to our regret; but we are left with the hope that she is saved, too, as this fascinating woman surely deserved to be.

The exotic woman we meet in Luke 7:31–48 is equally fascinating. Jesus's convivial nature, his willingness to attend feasts and dinners with a wide variety of worldly people, had attracted comment and censure by the pious. Jesus answered them, the religious establishment whom he termed "the men of this generation," through a curious metaphor: "They are like unto children sitting in the marketplace, and calling one to another, and saying, We have piped unto you, and ye have not danced; we have mourned to you, and ye have not wept." He said that John the Baptist ate neither bread nor wine, but the religious men complained, "He hath a devil." Jesus told them, "The Son of man is come eating and drinking; and ye say, Behold a gluttonous man, and a winebibber, a friend of publicans and sinners." He then added, mysteriously, "But wisdom is justified of all her children." All the same, a prominent Pharisee called Simon asked him to dinner, and Jesus agreed to come. News of the feast got around. "And behold," says Luke, "a woman in the city, which was a sinner, when she knew that Jesus sat at meat in the Pharisee's house, brought an alabaster box of ointment. And stood at his feet behind him weeping, and began to wash his feet with tears, and did wipe them with the hairs of her head, and kissed his feet, and anointed them with the ointment."

This was an extraordinary scene, for to wash a man's feet was a gesture of unusual humility in the ancient Near East, highly symbolic of submission and devotion. Jesus was to do it to his disciples shortly before his Crucifixion, provoking acute embarrassment on Peter's part. There must have been embarrassment on this occasion, too. For to wash a man's feet with tears, and dry them with your hair, was a supremely difficult feat, even if the tears were copious and the hair very long.

Moreover, the woman was beautiful and notorious. The Pharisee Simon was mortified. How had the woman got in? And did Jesus know about her? He "spake within himself, saying, This man, if he were a prophet, would have known who and what manner of woman this is that toucheth him."

Jesus read his thoughts and answered them: "Simon, I have somewhat to say unto thee." Simon replied, "Master, say on." Whereupon Jesus characteristically asked him a question: If a man had two creditors, one of five hundred pence, one of fifty, and forgave both, which of them would love him more? Simon said, "I suppose that he, to whom he forgave most." Exactly, said Jesus. Now he administered a rebuke: not angrily but in measured tones and careful words. "Seest thou this woman? I entered into thine house. Thou gavest me no water for my feet: but she hath washed my feet with tears, and wiped them with the hairs of her head. Thou gavest me no kiss: but this woman since I came in hath not ceased to kiss my feet. My head with oil thou didst not anoint: but this woman hath anointed my feet with ointment."

He then added, with some emphasis, "Wherefore I say unto thee, Her sins, which are many, are forgiven; for she loved much." To the woman he said, "Thy sins are forgiven." We do not hear any more about the woman, who—like the much-married Samaritan lady—disappears into unrecorded history, but not without Jesus's blessing: "Thy faith hath saved thee; go in peace." The lesson was lost on Simon and his friends. All they could say was "Who is this that forgiveth sins also?" But the repentant woman saved by faith, sublime in her humility, remains one of the most touching figures in ancient literature. And, as often in the New Testament, the matter-of-fact account by Luke has the resounding ring of truth.

This episode is an example of the extraordinary effect Jesus had on women. He evoked not only their faith and devotion but also an added dimension of tenderness tinged with poetry of gesture and sometimes of speech. The pagan Canaanite woman described in Matthew 15:22–28, who wanted Jesus to cure her daughter, was treated rather brusquely—she seems to have been persistent and importunate and was no doubt making a great noise. Jesus said his mission in Tyre and Sidon was to recover "the lost sheep of the house of Israel" and told her, "It is not meet to take the children's bread, and to cast it to dogs." Unabashed by this uncompromising reply, she was inspired to say, "Truth, Lord: yet the dogs eat of the crumbs which fall from the master's table." Instantly moved by this brilliant riposte, Jesus gave in: "O woman, great is thy faith: be it unto thee even as thou wilt." The daughter "was made whole from that very hour."

Jesus was conspicuous for gentleness, patience, and forbearance. He was hugely intuitive. He disliked any kind of legalism or ponderous logic, preferring the flashes of instant perception and poetry which illuminated his speech and turned his sayings into strings of sparkling jewels. These were not masculine characteristics. He relied more on emotions than reason to get across a point, a more feminine trait than what women expected from a preacher of doctrine. But then he was not a preacher: that was one thing women liked about him. He taught: he explained in an interesting, luminous way difficult things by using images from everyday life and work. He was a moralist but a poetical one. And Jesus was glad to make them interested and happy. He loved the two sisters of Lazarus who lived in Bethany, Martha and Mary, and clearly spent many precious hours there on the rare occasions when he rested. He knew well the sterling virtues of Martha and the staunchness of her faith—did she not make a declaration of it in terms which equaled in robustness the splendid confession of St. Peter? (Jn 11:27). But he liked Mary to sit at his feet and listen, and would not have her pleasure and instruction interrupted by household drudgery—"Mary hath chosen that good part," he freely admitted (Lk 10:42). "Let her alone," he said, when Judas Iscariot wanted to take away the alabaster jar of spikenard which she poured over his feet, "and the house was filled with the odour of the ointment" (Jn 12:2–8).

One reason Mary listened so intently was that the religion he outlined was quite different from Mosaic Judaism. Women were put right at the center of it alongside men, sharing equally in its duties and consolations. His mother, Mary, was an indispensable part of his Incarnation—his mission would have been impossible without her. The Holy Family to which he and she and his foster father Joseph belonged was, to him, the ideal image of the unit of society. To protect the family, he changed Mosaic law in one important particular: he placed marriage on an altogether higher plane of sanctity and made it indissoluble (Mt 19:5–6). A married couple were "one flesh": "What therefore God hath joined together let not man put asunder." Jesus's object in this unqualified condemnation of divorce was not merely to strengthen marriage but to protect women. Their inferior legal position in the ancient Near East was enhanced immeasurably by the ease with which men—but men only— could get a divorce. This applied everywhere in varying degrees. The penal code of Babylon laid down: "If a husband say unto his wife, Thou art not my wife, he shall pay half a mina and be free. But if a woman repudiate her husband, she shall be drowned in the river." Judaic law was less oppressive, but the school of Hillel declared it a sufficient ground for divorce if the wife had spoiled her husband's dinner. Other systems in Greece, Persia, and Rome, for instance, were not essentially different in treating the woman as inferior and a species of property. Even today, easy divorce bears harder on the wife than on the husband, and in upholding marriage, Jesus was the first teacher in world history to show his anxiety to put women on an equal footing with men.

It is true that Jesus selected only men for his apostolate. That was inevitable in the social conditions of the time, for his apostles were expected to go on independent missions, often alone, and to direct the disciples as part of the organization Jesus set up to spread his Gospel. Moreover, Jesus needed men to protect him from the hysteria of crowds and the physical threats of his enemies—not that they proved effective when it came to the end. It is one of the lessons of the life of Jesus that women often show more physical courage than men. He also expected his apostles to devote themselves full-time to his service. As Luke says, "they forsook all and followed him" (5:11). Peter states emphatically, "Lo, we have left all and have followed thee" (Mk 10:28). Virtually all women were not in a position to do this, at least formally, though it is clear some women contrived to manage it in practice. Jesus did not make a particular virtue of celibacy, though there is a passage in Matthew in which, contrary to traditional Jewish teaching, he showed it was lawful (19:10–12). He indicated it was a special calling: "He that is able to receive it, let him receive it." What Jesus did stress, time and again, was that devotion to God came before any family tie—father, mother, brother, sister. This applied equally to men and women. The notion of celibate monks or nuns living in communities is not incompatible with anything Jesus says in the Gospel. Nor is an all-male priesthood. But, equally, there is nothing in Jesus's teaching which rules out women priests.

What Jesus taught, essentially, is that friendship with God meant participation in a heavenly family which superseded all human ties, while not necessarily excluding them. Luke records a woman shouting out to Jesus from the crowd, "Blessed is the womb that bare thee, and the paps which thou hast sucked." Jesus agreed with her, but pointed to the higher value: "Yea rather, blessed are they that hear the word of God, and keep it" (11:27–29). There is an important passage in Matthew in which Jesus indicated that for the purpose of his mission on earth he was creating an apostolic family which necessarily had first place in his attention and affection. While he was teaching, his entourage told him that his mother and other members of his family, probably cousins, were waiting to speak to him. He answered, characteristically, with a question: "Who is my mother? and who are my brethren?" He answered it himself by a gesture toward his disciples: "Behold my mother and my brethren! For whosoever shall do the will of my Father which is in heaven, the same is my brother, and sister, and mother" (12:46–50). The most common word Jesus applies to God is "Father" and to himself is "Son." Human beings were first, and primarily, "children of God." That was the eternal relationship, outside time. Marriage, progeny, and human love within the family were all-important in worldly terms. Still, they were of this world: it was membership in God's family which mattered in the end.

In Jesus's family on earth, which he carefully composed and instructed, women were as numerous, though not perhaps as prominent, as men. His mother and other female members of her family were often present, and she was with him at the end, by the cross. Luke refers to a group of fallen women, whom Jesus had cured of their "devils"—that is, their licentiousness—and recruited for his entourage (8:2). The most important of them was Mary Magdalene, and Luke emphasizes the sinfulness of her former life by saying "out of whom went seven devils." Then there were Martha and Mary, the sisters of Lazarus. But Luke also mentions a group of well-to-do women, which included Joanna, the wife of Herod Antipas's steward Chuza, and Susanna. These are the only two he names, but he says there were "many others." They "ministered unto him of their substance" (8:3). Jesus's traveling mission needed financial support as well as servicing, and this was primarily supplied by women. The first echelon, the apostles, were all men. But the second group, responsible for housing and meals and traveling expenses, were women, usually of ample means. Jesus had the ability, partly because of his character, partly through the appeal of his teaching, to attract intelligent, educated, cultured, and sensitive women, who found in his words a kind of religion infinitely more moving and satisfying than anything they could get in the synagogue or Temple. This appeal to affluent women was not confined to Jewish or Samaritan circles. The wife of Pilate, the governor of Judaea, was also fascinated with Jesus. She could not join his entourage, of course, but she had dreams about him and tried to persuade her husband to save him: "Have thou nothing to do with that just man: for I have suffered many things this day in a dream because of him" (Mt 27:19). The other affluent ladies were also prevented by their situation from going on missionary work, but they provided the means to sustain it and came to help when Jesus and his disciples were within range of their homes. The widows could work with him full-time. These women foreshadowed the Roman ladies who, in the early days of Christianity, flocked to the catacombs and the first churches and were, in great part, responsible for its spread and success. Jesus's teaching was such that a woman could identify herself with it absolutely, and the higher her rank and the more independent minded she was, the stronger the bonds with the Master. Prostitutes, whose profession itself was a form of emancipation, were also violently attracted the moment they forsook their degrading way of life.

That Jesus loved the society of women, felt at home with them, and knew how to talk to and respond to them is clear from the Gospel. But he also loved children. It was one of his most marked and powerful characteristics. He saw in children uncorrupted innocence before the material attractions of the sinful world distorted the instinct of purity and love. He liked children of all ages. Young mothers sensed his love of babies and handed their own to him to caress. There is a striking passage in Mark which illustrates Jesus's ability to be comfortable with the very young, which makes him unique (so far as I know) in the literature of the ancient world: "[T]hey brought young children to him, that he should touch them." The disciples, more typical of their times, did not like this and rebuked the mothers. "But when Jesus saw it, he was much displeased, and said unto them, Suffer the little children to come unto me, and forbid them not: for of such is the kingdom of God." He often compared children with the sinless and now, inspired by this attempt to deny him their company, summed up his feelings: "Verily I say unto you, Whosoever shall not receive the kingdom of God as a little child, he shall not enter therein." To emphasize his point, he "took them up in his arms, put his hands upon them, and blessed them" (10:13–16). Matthew 19:13–14 recounts the same incident, adding, "[O]f such is the kingdom of heaven."

The theme that a certain childish innocence was required even of grown men and women to fit souls for salvation was one which recurred frequently in Jesus's teaching. It was linked to his image of being "born again" and to his love of humility. But Jesus loved the child not just as an image but as a reality.

He was fascinated by every aspect of the way in which a baby comes into the world and then grows and becomes a delightful child. He brought them into his teaching constantly. He was very observant. He noted how the delight of a mother in her baby obliterated the pains of childbirth (Jn 16:21), how the father cuddled his child in bed (Lk 11:7), and how parents listened to what children said and granted their requests, but only when unharmful (Mt 7:9; Lk 11:11–13). The impulses of children at play interested him (Mt 11:16) and so did their sorrows (Mt 18:25). He regarded as the supreme test of loyalty the willingness of a disciple to leave his children for his, and God's, sake (Lk 14:26, 18:29; Mt 19:29). For Jesus, the love of husband and wife for each other and their shared love of their children are inextricably intermingled, and part of the intimate way in which human love can imitate and foreshadow the love which is the sustaining principle of God's Kingdom.

Unwilling as Jesus was to perform miracles for show, he invariably acted when begged by a parent to heal a sick child. It is notable how large a proportion of his cures benefited children. The little child of the nobleman at Capernaum (Jn 4:49); the distressed boy (Mt 17:18), "the only child of his father," whom Jesus healed while descending from the mountain; Jairus's "little daughter" (Mk 5:23), whom Jesus raised from death; the "daughter" of the Canaanite woman (Mk 7:30); and the only son of the widow of Nain (Lk 7:11–18) are only some of the cases where Jesus hastened to the aid of a sorrow-ing parent. Life was cheap in first-century Palestine. Children died all around him of neglect and poverty as well as disease. But when a particular case of a suffering child was placed be-fore him, he always acted. He preached not only "Feed my sheep" but also, markedly, "Feed my lambs."

Moreover, Jesus was always prepared to remind people, even his instructed followers, that children were not to be ig-nored. In some ways they were models. When his disciples held their unseemly dispute as to which of them was the greatest, an incident recorded in all three synoptics (Mt 18:1–4; Mk 9:33–37; Lk 9:46–48), Jesus called to him a child and placed it in their midst, saying, "Except ye be converted, and become as little children, ye shall not enter into the kingdom of heaven." It was always Jesus's teaching, and his profound belief, that the study of children had much to tell. Matthew records the delight he felt when, in his last days on earth, children in the Temple greeted him with hosannas, and the way in which he rebuked the officials who protested against the salutation as unseemly: "Yea; have ye never read, Out of the mouths of babes and sucklings thou hast perfected praise?" (21:16). It is also remarkable that Jesus reserved his fiercest warnings for those who ill-treated children or led them into wickedness. Matthew quotes him as saying, "Take heed that ye despise not one of my little ones" (18:10), and "[W]hoso shall offend one of these little ones which believe in me, it were better for him that a millstone were hanged about his neck, and that he were drowned to the depth of the sea" (18:6).

If women and children had special plans in Jesus's heart and his notions of innocence and virtue, what of the aged? Almost inevitably, many of his healings—only a handful are specifically described—benefited old people. The hopeless cripple who had hung about the pool of Bethesda for nearly forty years was obviously old. So was the woman with "an issue of blood," who had for many years spent all her money on doctors without finding a cure. Jesus noticed virtuous old people, like the widow who put her two mites into the collection box. But he was careful not to attribute particular merit merely to the aged. Orthodox Judaism already did that, and Jesus was not impressed. The status of "rulers" in the synagogues and at the Temple was based partly on seniority, and age was important at every level of the sacerdotal hierarchy. A specific term, "elder," paid tribute to age in Judaism. Jesus thought them to be often elders in sin. In an important passage in Matthew, Jesus said that publicans and prostitutes would go to heaven before the elders (21:31–32). At the time Jesus was born, saintly old men like Simeon and Zacharias were to be found constantly at the Temple. But by the time Jesus completed his ministry there were no good old men in its precincts. Joseph Caiaphas, the head priest, had been many years in his post and must have been in his late fifties at least. His father-in-law, Annas, formerly the high priest and the power behind the scenes, was even older. Many of the orthodox Jews who listened to Jesus in the hope of catching him out, or to report back any blasphemous sayings, were old; some were technically elders. The establishment against which Jesus so often protested was essentially run by old men. Hence his sayings that to enter God's Kingdom it was necessary to be "born again" and to become "a new man" were double-edged. Jesus's use of the child image for the saved and his stress on the blessed being "children of God" were both so frequent and so important in his imagery that there is a distinct impression in the New Testament, taken as a whole, that age had somehow to be annihilated or transformed in the quest for God.

This impression is powerfully reinforced by the Transfiguration, one of the most remarkable events described in the Gospels. A few days before he was transfigured, Jesus had questioned his disciples about what men said of his mission. Peter answered, "Thou art Christ, the son of the living God." Jesus then made him in effect his deputy and vicar, and pronounced him blessed: "[F]lesh and blood have not revealed it unto thee but my Father which is in heaven. And I say also unto thee, That thou art Peter, and upon this rock I will build my church; and the gates of hell shall not prevail against it" (Mt 16:15–20). Six days later he took Peter, with James and John, "up into an high mountain apart, And he was transfigured before them:

and his face did shine as the sun, and his raiment was white as the light" (Mt 17:1–2). Both Mark 9:2–8 and Luke 9:28–36 also record this spectacular irradiation of Jesus's face and body. All three describe a divine epiphany. Matthew puts it thus: "[A] bright cloud overshadowed them: and behold a voice out of the cloud, which said, This is my beloved Son, in whom I am well pleased; hear ye him" (17:5).

The Transfiguration has been variously interpreted. But its meaning seems clear. Jesus was a man, but not only a man. He was also God, Son of the Father. He was living outside time and space, as well as upon earth. His ministry was taking place not only in this world but also in the next. What he said was true for all time, in earthly reckoning but also for eternity. It was being put before men in a small province of the Roman Empire during the early part of the first century AD, but its truth applied to all peoples, at all times, transfiguring history and geography, spreading everywhere and bridging the gulf between the universe God created and the infinite in which he had his being.

Over the next two thousand years, the changes which Jesus first introduced among human beings would slowly revolutionize society, so that his transfiguration on the high mountain was a foretaste of a gradual modification of attitudes and mentalities.

VII

✝ Jesus's New Ten
Commandments

THE AIM OF JESUS was not to change the world. His aim was to fit its inhabitants for the Kingdom of God, which he insisted "is not of this world." The ancient Hebrews were confused about this life and the next and only gradually, and imperfectly, learned to embrace a concept of the hereafter. In Jesus's day, many Jews, such as the Sadducees, still refused to accept the concept of an afterlife. So it is not strange that the belief in "the Christ" or Messiah or savior or redeeming King of Israel, which was prevalent in Jesus's day, was muddled. Virtually all Jews believed in it, in varying degrees of intensity. So did the Samaritans—the woman Jesus met at the well, who had had five husbands and was now living in sin, may not have been squeamish about morals, but she knew all about the Christ and was delighted to recognize Jesus as such. But neither Jews nor Samaritans were sure whether the Messiah was a secular leader or a spiritual leader or a bit of both. The Sadducees saw him as another David who would restore the great Jewish kingdom which had flourished a thousand years before. The Pharisees saw him as a theocratic high priest who would make the Temple the seat of government.

Jesus inherited the doctrine of the Messiah but not the confusions. As the Son of God he never had the smallest doubt that "my Father's business," as he put it, was to show all who would listen how to make themselves fit for the next world. He demanded not allegiance as another David, or a secular ruler, or even a theocratic priest-king, but faith as a spiritual leader whose power and Kingdom lay in eternity. He insisted he was not a revolutionary or a Zealot or a rebel against Rome or even against the Jewish authorities. He took no steps to disturb the political status quo. But no one quite believed him, not even his disciples. The apostles themselves were unsure what would be the end of his ministry. They found it hard to accept that he was a sacrificial victim who would die for humanity. And these were devout men in daily contact with Jesus. The further people were from his person, the less they knew about his teaching, the more suspicious they were. The men of the Temple establishment had no doubt that Jesus was a troublemaker who envied their positions and planned to usurp them, a rabble-rouser who would embroil them in a destructive conflict with the Roman power, which terrified them. The idea of a leader-teacher whose concepts and aims were entirely spiritual was something beyond their worldly conception.

Jesus himself always strove to draw absolute distinctions between heaven and earth. He was not concerned with political arrangements or even political philosophy. He was aware that in AD 6 there had been a "tumult" in Palestine and Syria over the great census, which had led to bloodshed when the Roman occupation forces put it down. Census was for tax purposes, "tribute" as it was called. Jesus knew that his ecclesiastical enemies, the "Temple men," would try to embroil him in political disputes about the tribute. It was so easy to present him to the Roman authorities as a tax rebel who tried to persuade the people not to pay tribute. That was the specific charge that the Temple men brought against Jesus when they finally got him before Pilate's judgment seat: "We found this fellow perverting the nation, and forbidding to give tribute to Caesar, saying that he himself is Christ a King" (Lk 23:2). This was a deliberate lie. Jesus had gone out of his way *not* to forbid tribute. The Pharisees and the supporters of Herod Antipas had tried to trap him into making such a mistake. They insinuated, in words Matthew records, that he was a fearless critic of existing authority who only spoke the truth: "[N]either carest thou for any man: for thou regardest not the person of men. Tell us therefore, What thinkest thou? Is it lawful to give tribute unto Caesar, or not?" But Jesus "perceived their wickedness, and said: Why tempt you me, ye hypocrites?" He demanded they produce a coin, and when they did so, asked, "Whose is this image and superscription?" They said, "Caesar's." He told them, "Render therefore unto Caesar the things which are Caesar's, and to God the things that are God's." This masterly retort silenced them. "They marvelled, and went their way" (22:16–22).

The metaphor of the coin was typical of Jesus's efforts to show that his teaching drew absolute distinctions between the material and the spiritual, between this world and the next. He came not to liberate the Jews from the Romans but to show all human beings how to liberate themselves from sin. His object was not to found a new regime but to portray a new way of life. The revolution was entirely inward, a revolution against selfishness and greed, cruelty and prejudice, anger and lust: a revolution from self-love into love for all and fellowship with everyone. The reborn person would be totally different, and all would be changed. But outwardly, the world would carry on.

Or would it? The key to the life of Jesus is a huge paradox: the most striking and important paradox in world history. Jesus aimed to show men and women how to prepare themselves for the next world, to make themselves worthy of it. But he did so with such grace and skill, such psychological and emotional brilliance, that he also gave them a pattern to follow which made them better, and therefore happier, human beings in the present world. At the heart of Christianity is the imitation of Christ. The Gospels show how the perfect person behaves and thinks and speaks. By imitating Christ to the best of their limited abilities, those who have followed him over two thousand years have made the world a better place, and they have enabled many of those who dwell in it to lead more fulfilled and happier lives. The quest for the next world has transformed this one. But Jesus's example, though the most powerful and pervasive, has not been the only force at work. Humanity has a propensity for evil as well as good. And other imposing figures in history have set a bad example and written and spoken words that have misled and perverted many. I write in the early part of the twenty-first century, and as a historian I can survey two millennia of changes in which the example of Jesus has battled for the minds of men and women against what he would have called the forces of darkness. There have been great epochs of transformation among the civilized: the rise of Christendom in Europe, its triumph, and its decay; the Renaissance and Reformation; the first scientific revolution of the seventeenth century; the Enlightenment of the eighteenth century; the Industrial Revolution and the advent of sensibility and reform; the colossal intellectual and social changes of the twentieth century, which continue in our own epoch. All these have been a combination of good and evil, of justice and savagery, of tenderness and cruelty, of progress and degeneration. But if we sort out the salutary aspects from the deplorable, if we look at what is decent and valuable in our modern sensibilities— now, in the second decade of the twenty-first century—we see that all the genuine improvements in the way human beings live

and behave toward one another spring from following the teaching and, above all, the example of Jesus.

What Jesus provided by his life was in effect a new Ten
Commandments. A close study of the Gospels, such as I have
tried to reflect in this brief biography, shows us what they are.
The first is: each of us must develop a true personality. Jesus
taught that each of us is unique, and that each has, in addition
to a body, a soul in which our character is preserved. The body
is frail and mortal; the soul is indestructible and timeless. This
is Jesus's most important teaching, which is implied in all his
remarks. We have a duty to become self-conscious: not in any
egotistical sense but by becoming aware of our existence as an
act of God's creation. We may have all kinds of collective ex-
istences, as a member of a family, a tribe, a nation, a race, a
religious group, or a profession. But our personality, as we shape
it and carry it, stands absolutely alone in the face of God. He
knows everything about us, and sees and weighs everything we
do, say, and think. Our knowledge of this is a key element in
our self-consciousness. But linked to our awareness of ourselves is the right to self-determination. Each has a will, and it
is by the exercise of this will that we shape the personality which
is given to us at birth and belongs to us throughout our lives.
However insignificant and impotent any of us may appear to
be, we all have a will which is free, and therefore possess a right
and an ability to exercise self-determination which is absolute.

The personality is, or can be, all-powerful over itself, and it is always unfettered. That is what St. Paul meant when, within a generation of Jesus's death, he wrote that "where the Spirit of the Lord is, there is liberty" (2 Cor 3:17).

The social and political implications of personality are infinite and become the essence of Christianity. They have been worked out over two thousand years of history, and are still being worked out today. Personality, human uniqueness, is the glory of the human race. But it has implications. First, accountability: we alone are responsible for the personality as we shape it in life. And we will be held accountable for it at death. The last judgment, and its implications for eternity, is the price we pay for self-determination. Second, though each personality is unique it is also incomplete. The soul is given by God and has an ineradicable impulse to return to its Creator. It cannot be at rest until this is accomplished. By free will, this becomes possible. If the personality we are given but which we also help to shape is finally acceptable, we enter what Jesus called "the Kingdom." If it is not, we are refused. Jesus spoke of this repeatedly, using a variety of metaphors. He made it plain that earning acceptance of the personality we shape is the object of life on earth. Nonacceptance entails punishment: what St. Thomas Aquinas calls "the pain of loss," using the similes of losing and finding which abound in Jesus's teaching.

Thus personality is the key to life. Jesus made this clear

when he said, "For whosoever will save his life shall lose it; but whosoever shall lose his life for my sake and the gospel's, the same shall save it. For what shall it profit a man, if he shall gain the whole world, and lose his own soul?" (Mk 8:35–36).

The second commandment is: accept, and abide by, universality. The consistent, daily, unremitting implication of Jesus's teaching is to see the human race as a whole. Each soul is unique, but each is part of humanity. Here, as often, Jesus draws an absolute distinction between the material and the spiritual. The difference between one personality and another, one soul and another, may be infinite. The material difference between one body and another, when compared with their essential similarities, is insignificant. We are all neighbors in the eyes of God, and we must all become neighbors in our own eyes. Jesus's doctrine of the neighbor, most strikingly illustrated in his parable of the Good Samaritan, is overt or implicit in everything he said or did. Politically and socially it is a very powerful doctrine. Jesus never set himself up as a pacifist or a democrat, or a multi-racialist or a humanitarian. Insofar as any of these creeds are valid he belonged to all of them. For him, the love of God implied that you loved your neighbor as yourself, and once you accepted that, the practice of it—the "Great Commandment," as he called it—embraced all the felicitous arrangements which mankind's ingenuity has contrived to bring people together in universal harmony. Neighborliness is a wonderful commandment. It is a principle everyone can understand. It applies to all circumstances. And it is not essentially difficult—albeit harder than we think at times, and with particular neighbors.

The third commandment is: respect the fact that we are all equal in God's eyes. Striving to be first was something Jesus found distasteful. He knew that human beings tended to form themselves into hierarchies, but he disliked seeing the results. When his disciples, even his apostles, quarreled about priorities among themselves, he was grieved. He shuddered at pushiness. When prominent elders or rulers of the synagogue strove for higher places on the benches he turned away in disgust. He warned against those who took top seats at the table. He never missed an opportunity to disparage the insensitivity of the rich and the kings of the world, or to praise the humble and lowly in spirit. The repeated refrain of his Gospel was "the first shall be last; and the last shall be first" (Mt 19:30). It was not that Jesus despised effort and industry or failed to recognize ability. Much of his teaching, and many of his parables, praised those who tried hard and well. The "good and faithful servant" was a noble figure for him. But so was the poor widow with her two mites. To Jesus the human race was a vast, moving mass trudging its way across time and space, evoking his pity and sympathy not only in its endless sufferings, often self-inflicted, but also in its secret heroism—a mass by virtue of its numbers, but actually composed of countless individuals, each precious to God, meriting equality of treatment according to deserts, and receiving it from his judicious hands, directed by his all-seeing eyes. The best that human beings could do—and this applied particularly to rulers or officials, anyone given power by birth or ability or money or chance—was to try to follow God's example and give equal consideration to all. Thus equality, as Jesus taught it, was not an abstract doctrine but a living practice.

He also taught—and this is the fourth commandment—the need for love in human relationships, at all times and in every situation. "Love" was a word often on his lips, whether it be the love of God or the love of other human beings. This love had nothing to do with lust, which was a form of self-love, but neither was it entirely disembodied or spiritual. It was emotional, binding body and spirit, and expressing itself in countless ways. What Jesus tried to do, in his life and ministry, was to show love in action: in noticing, in listening, in questioning, in comforting and helping, in curing and making whole, in uniting and reconciling, in all the activities of a busy teacher's life but also in private conversations and even secret encounters. The four Gospels form an exemplary manual of love, culminating in what Jesus himself classified as the greatest act of love, the giving of one's own life for others. You cannot lay down laws of love. What you can do is to show it. That is what Jesus did. Happily, his words and actions were recorded in the multifocus vision for four very different evangelists. So we have a pattern to follow. And in the study and imitation of Jesus we have the best means to carry out his fourth commandment.

The fifth commandment of Jesus's life concerns mercy. We are to show mercy just as God shows it to us. It is an emotional word, like "love"—with which it is intimately connected. It is hard to define, though instantly recognizable when exercised. It is something which cannot be done to excess and is significant even in its minutest expression. Mercy is grace. It is undeserved. It is something we pray for and give thanks for. Jesus says that if you get the glorious chance to show mercy, do so, without forethought or afterthought, without reason or logic, not expecting thanks or even repentance, not to accomplish something in the way of social or personal reform, simply for its own sake. Jesus was not a man to compose perfect codes of law or a Universal Declaration of Human Rights. The idea of the Rights of Man was alien to him. He did not believe in Rights, or even in rights. He was more inclined to believe in duties, though not in Duties. Mercy transcended all these categories. No one had a right to it. And by its nature it was exercised freely, not as a duty. It was a marvelous thing: a form of moral poetry. When we show mercy spontaneously, gladly, freely, instantly, not thoughtlessly but unthinkingly and happily, we behave not just in kingly fashion but like God himself—it is the best way to show we are made in his image. Jesus was familiar with two texts from the book of Ecclesiasticus: "For the

Lord is full of compassion and mercy, longsuffering, and very pitiful, and forgiveth sins" (2:11) and "We will fall into the hands of the Lord, and not into the hands of men: for as his majesty is, so is his mercy" (2:18). However, Jesus in his New Testament was aiming to complete and replace the old: to make his new commandments immediate and relevant and exciting. So he sought to make human beings exercise mercy after the manner of a king, and of God himself. And in doing so he had an impact, over the following two millennia, greater than that of any code, or treatise, or jurisprudence, on the way those who err are treated by their fellow men and women. In the crown of modernity, mercy is one of the brightest jewels among societies which have earned the right to wear it.

Jesus pushed virtues like mercy as far as they could go, but he was not an extremist. On the contrary, all the evidence of the Gospels shows the balance of his life, the faultless way in which he steered sensibly between egregious positions. He was a private man but not a hermit. He could be solitary but only for brief periods. He liked company in moderation. He talked— he had much to say—but he said it succinctly, and he knew when to ask questions and when to be silent. He was equable but could express indignation when required. He could weep, but he never despaired. He could laugh—though we are never explicitly told so—but he laughed with, not at. He was mocked, but he never mocked. He was struck, and he turned the other cheek. In an age of fury and loathing, when religious extrem-ism held sway, he was a difficult man to dislike, let alone hate. And if, in the end, the unbalanced men hated him enough to kill him, it was precisely for his equanimity. A careful reading of the Gospels shows us the man who always kept his head (if not his life) when others were losing theirs. They teach us patience, forbearance, self-control, calmness, serenity, the pur-suit and maintenance of quiet amid the storms of life. For more than two thousand years this has proved a valuable lesson to those individuals and societies intelligent enough to learn it.

Balance, then, is the sixth new commandment. And it is linked to the seventh: the cultivation of an open mind. Jesus's life and death were a struggle against those whose minds were closed. He disliked bigotry in any form and spoke out against it constantly. It was to be found among the religious establish-ment of his day: the Temple men especially, and the leaders of the sects, such as the Pharisees and Sadducees. Bigotry sprang from legalism, adherence to the letter of the law and its narrow-minded interpretation. It is significant that Jesus's listeners said he spoke in exactly the opposite way to the scribes. They meant he was constantly using his eyes and his wits, his imagination and his intelligence, to take in fresh knowledge. Luke quotes him exclaiming, "Woe unto you, lawyers, for ye have taken away the key of knowledge" (11:52). Jesus kept his eyes open to take in what he saw in daily life, and his ears open to listen to what men and women said. That was essentially linked to a mind open to new experiences and ideas. The word "open," like "light," was blessed in his vocabulary. He commended it to humanity. In the two millennia since he was crucified, the world has improved itself insofar as it has kept its mind open. All the ameliorative aspects of the early church, in its overthrow of paganism; Christianity, in all its attempts to create a truly religious society; the Renaissance, in its recovery of what was best in antiquity; the Reformation, in its redemption of apostolic virtue; the scientific revolution, in its adoption of experiment and verification; the Enlightenment, in its quest for exact knowledge; and modern reformist societies, in their seeking to improve the lot of humble men, women, and children, have succeeded when their leaders kept open minds and failed when they succumbed to dogma and "correctness."

Jesus constantly emphasized that dogmatic beliefs, bigotry, and the insistence that there is only one "correct" way of doing, thinking, and talking—as prevalent in his society as in ours—are the exact opposite of truth. The pursuit of truth, whole and unabridged, simple and pure, unadorned by sectarian usage, unstained by passion, is the most valuable of human activities. It is the eighth new commandment. "Truth" is another key word in Jesus's vocabulary: "I am the way, the truth, and the life" (Jn 14:6). The saying cannot be too often quoted and pondered. The truth is both God's truth and truth in nature. Truth is found by going God's way, and with the grain of the natural world, not against it. Jesus loved the natural world. That is one reason why, when he wanted to think intensely and pray most earnestly, he went into the desert or up into the mountains, where nature is at its most severe and in its raw state. A huge range of his images were taken directly from nature. It formed the parameters of his poetry. Nature, in whole and in part, was the metaphor of his discourse. It was created, and therefore in a sense sacred. All was minutely and affectionately cataloged in God's providence: "Are not five sparrows sold for two farthings, and not one of them is forgotten before God?" (Lk 12:6). Jesus loved nature because he loved truth, and to go against nature was to defy the truth. It followed that all human enterprises should go with the grain of nature, not against it. He saw nature as providential, orderly, satisfying, and beautiful, and his constant references to the growth of organic things (Mk 4:18, 26–28, 31ff., 13:28; Lk 13:8, 21; Jn 15:2–4) and the habits of animals (Mt 6:26, 7:15, 10:16; Lk 13:34; Jn 10:3–5, 10:12) testify to his love of watching the creative regularity of God expressing itself in the natural world. For humans to recklessly and senselessly damage nature, whether organic or inorganic, was to trespass. It was for humanity to inhabit, use, preserve, and protect the world as God intended in his providential plan. That was the meaning of truth to nature, and being true to nature is the eighth new commandment.

The ninth new commandment concerns power, its exercise, and the respect due to the powerless. Jesus had at his disposal limitless power and, as his conduct during the temptations and thereafter throughout his ministry showed, he was careful always to exercise it with restraint and moderation, with mercy, pity, and love. His life is a model of the judicious use of power and, by contrast, his death is a cruel and catastrophic example of its abuse. Everything to do with power is rehearsed in the life and death of Jesus, and he himself, first in his miracles and then in his sufferings, is the archetype of the all-powerful and the powerless. In the thousands of years since he lived and died, the rulers of the earth and those who suffer from their distortions of power have been able to turn to the Gospels for a message of guidance, on the one hand, and hope, on the other. The Crucifixion is the nemesis of worldly power, and the Resurrection is the upsurge of the powerless from the depths. No handbook of political theory, no blueprint for the distribution and use of power, no analysis of its abuses or plan for their avoidance or correction, can add anything substantial to the story of Jesus and power, as told by the evangelists. What we need to know, and avoid, is all to be found therein, and any set of political and constitutional arrangements which does not place respect for the powerless at its center is bound to offend against truth and love.

The tenth and last of the new commandments, which we find in Jesus's words, actions, and sufferings, is: show courage. The particular form of courage which Jesus displayed, and exhorted his followers to show, is courage not merely in resisting but in enduring wrong. He called his disciples to a life of meekness—that is, restrained strength, the high courage of endurance of pain and persecution, a sustained heroism in the face of iniquity, and a dogged persistence in proclaiming the truth at all costs. Jesus told his followers: "In your patience possess ye your souls" (Lk 21:19) and "[Y]e shall be hated of all men for my name's sake: but he that endureth to the end shall be saved" (Mt 10:22). Jesus expected his followers to show courage, and he showed it himself: the special courage of one who knows exactly the suffering ahead and is afraid of it, but accepts it nonetheless. He told his disciples to take up their crosses and showed how it ought to and could be done. Jesus was God and man, and the Crucifixion is the story of the exercise of divine courage in a frail human body. That is what we are commanded to aspire to, and this courage in imitation of Jesus is as much needed today as ever, and in as short supply as it was in his time. All the more reason, then, why this final commandment should be understood plainly, and followed faithfully.

The new commandments which Jesus left behind him were the moral and social framework of the Christianity he founded and his followers brought into existence—in all its better aspects, that is. Gradually, over the centuries, the salient virtues of the message Jesus conveyed to the people of his land percolated through society, leaving precious traces of love and neighborliness, mercy and forgiveness, courage in suffering and faith in goodness. In our own age, the early decades of the twenty-first century, we feel that our own society, ideally at least, is free and open, democratic and representative, living under a rule of law which is progressive and enlightened.

In fact, human progress has proved an illusion as often as not. In many ways our society is no better organized and led than in those weary days two millennia ago when men like Herod and Pilate ruled. Insofar as we have improved—in the way we look after the poor, the sick, the infirm, the powerless; in our treatment of children; in moral education and training; in penology and the redressing of grievances; in the effort to spread material welfare and to encourage people to show kindness to one another and help their neighbors in difficult times—these improvements have come about because we have had the sense, the sensibility, the intelligence, and the pertinacity to follow where Jesus led. If goodness has a place in our twenty-first-century world, it is because Jesus, by his words and actions, showed us how to put it there. No other man in history has had this effect over so long a time, over the whole of the earth's surface, and over such a range of issues.

But, of course, Jesus was God as well as man. We now turn to the tragic but ultimately glorious events which displayed his superhuman qualities and vindicated his divinity.

VIII

✝ Jesus's Trial and Crucifixion

T HE EVENTS LEADING UP to the Crucifixion of Jesus, as described in the four Gospels, were complicated, and it is not surprising there are minor discrepancies. One was written by an eyewitness, and the other three were based on eyewitnesses' observations. There is unanimity on all the essential points. This is remarkable, for there is more agreement in the sources about the death of Jesus than there is about the assassination of Julius Caesar in the Roman senate less than a century before, despite the fact that Caesar was a world-famous figure, and the senate house the governing center of the known universe. The death of Jesus the man is a tragic story. It is well authenticated in nearly all the details, and in describing it, I am conflating all four accounts to produce as complete and truthful a version as possible.

Jesus was, by his nature, the most successful religious teacher in antiquity. His appearance, his voice, his words, his unique combination of authority and gentleness, made him attractive to people of all ages, classes, and races. And he cured the sick, though usually privately and at their entreaty. He never used a cure for demonstrative ends. Still, his powers were there, and were known to be there. So almost from the first day of his ministry, he attracted the attention of the authorities, especially the religious ones. They feared him. They saw him as a threat to their positions and even their lives. The high priest Caiaphas, a devious and artful operator who hugely valued and enjoyed his power as spiritual leader of the orthodox Jewish community, got on very well with Pontius Pilate, the Roman governor of Judaea, and Herod Antipas, the leading secular Jewish petty king of the area, and he wanted to keep relations as they were. A Jewish popular preacher whom he did not control was a threat to his authority, and if his teaching turned out to be revolutionary, there could be a tumult, for which he would be blamed. As Jesus's fame spread, and the number of people he could attract increased, so the threat appeared to grow. News that he had persuaded more than five thousand people to ascend a mountain and hear him preach there, and then by a "miracle" fed them heartily with fishes and loaves, filled the ruling priests with terror. What if he did this in a city? Could he not then take it over by force? What if he did it in Jerusalem itself? Then he could occupy it, proclaim himself another King David, and become priest-king. The Romans would then pull out, except from the Antonia fortress, return with reinforcements from Syria in massive strength, take the city, massacre all its Jewish inhabitants, including and especially the priests, and raze it to the ground. They were quite capable of doing so; indeed, they had done so to other rebellious cities in their empire. The priests trembled for their lives as well as their jobs and property. And in a sense they were right to fear, for such a catastrophe actually occurred a generation later, about AD 70, and Jerusalem was taken; indeed, about 132, after a further tumult, it was literally destroyed, leaving not a stone standing erect. Yet they never made a serious effort to discover exactly what Jesus was teaching and quite how he saw his ministry reaching its climax. They periodically sent spies or agents provocateurs to get him to provide damaging verbal evidence to be used later to put him to death. But they never accepted his assurances that the Kingdom he spoke of was a spiritual one, not of this world. It was alien to their nature to recognize a holy man without worldly ambitions. They were corrupt and materialistic, unable to recognize spiritual goodness when they saw it. They did not exactly deny Jesus's power, but they claimed it was the work of the devil, just as the spiritual potentates of contemporary Iran call their opponents Satan.

Jesus certainly had no wish to challenge the high priesthood. For three years he made every effort to avoid a direct confrontation. He went to the populous centers of Judaea, and especially Jerusalem, only rarely, and then without display. He concealed or used only under pressing entreaty his powers. He begged those he healed not to boast about what had happened. He often taught in private houses or in the open countryside or by the shore of the Sea of Galilee, so as to provoke authority as little as possible. He never spoke against Roman rule—quite the contrary—and if he criticized Jewish leadership it was on spiritual grounds alone. Externally there was nothing revolutionary about him, a friendly, kindly figure telling people to be meek, praising humility, loving the poor, and asking all to turn the other cheek. What harm could he possibly do?

But in one sense he was a revolutionary. He asked for a revolution in the hearts of men and women—a turning from worldliness to spiritual life. And that was enough to cause a popular effervescence which in turn detonated the crisis. Moreover, though Jesus was always careful to avoid antagonizing the priests deliberately, he knew that his destiny was to be a sacrifice, and that his life would be lost by speaking the truth. He always did speak the truth—"I am the way, the truth, and the life" was his rule, his slogan, his motto, his manifesto—and he tended to speak it more clearly and vehemently as his ministry progressed. The religious leaders constantly planned to seize him and have him put to death. They would have done so on half a dozen occasions, but either Jesus slipped away before they could seize him or the crowds surrounding him were too enthusiastic and large to make it possible without a pitched battle, which they might have lost. The priests had an armed force of Temple guards, but it was a matter of argument whether they had the power, either secular or spiritual, to pronounce let alone carry out a death sentence. In John the Baptist's case they had been spared the trouble by the machinations of Herodias and the sinuous skills of her daughter Salome. Against Jesus they hoped to stir up an angry Jewish mob to stone him to death. But there was never much chance of that. He was too popular. It is true that the priests could, given sufficient warning, assemble a crowd of household servants, up to a thousand, who could carry out a public demonstration. In the end that is exactly what they did do. As they controlled the limited access to the forecourt of the governor's palace, the demonstration appeared effective. Modern experience teaches us how easily these official protests can be staged by the authorities.

Two events finally decided the priests to act, and made their action possible. Shortly before the Passover feast in the spring, Jesus raised from the dead his friend Lazarus, brother of Martha and Mary and a man well known and much loved among the community both in Bethany, where his home lay, and in Jerusalem. The texts suggest a certain reluctance on Jesus's part, though they do not actually say he deliberately delayed. As it turned out, Lazarus had been dead four days before Jesus arrived at his sealed tomb and shouted to him to come out. There could be no question that Lazarus's resurrection was a miraculous event. There were many witnesses both to his death and to his reappearance. There could have been no trickery and no other explanation than that a miraculous event had taken place. It was the talk of Jerusalem, and the priests were alarmed. Indeed, they finally made up their minds to take action against the man who could (in their view) summon Satan to his aid. They also planned to kill Lazarus before he could publicize what had happened to him.

The second event was Jesus's own decision that the time to make his sacrifice, for which he had been put on earth, had come, and to make a public entry into Jerusalem. There is a hint of this, earlier, in Luke: "And it came to pass, when the time was come that he should be received up, he stedfastly set his face to go to Jerusalem" (9:51). It was always especially dangerous for him to set foot in the city, and particularly so after the Lazarus affair. In St. John's account, which is the most specific about the chronology, he began Passion Week on Saturday, the Jewish Sabbath, by having supper at Lazarus's house with Martha, Mary, and other friends. Mary took "a pound of ointment of spikenard, very costly, and anointed the feet of Jesus, and wiped his feet with her hair: and the house was filled with the odour of the ointment." This deliberate reenactment of the charitable act of the sinful woman at the house of Simon the Pharisee aroused the anger of Judas Iscariot, the keeper of the funds used by the disciples. But when he said (being a thief, as John writes), "Why was not this ointment sold for three hundred pence, and given to the poor?" Jesus said, "Let her alone: against the day of my burying hath she kept this. For the poor always ye have with you; but me ye have not always" (Jn 12:3–8).

This hint of his approaching death was ignored, and the next day he and his party set off publicly to enter the big city. Everyone knew. The crowds were immense. Jesus sat on "a young ass," and the people "[t]ook branches of palm trees and went forth to meet him, and cried, Hosanna: Blessed is the King of Israel that cometh in the name of the Lord!" (Jn 12:13–14). Jesus, knowing his time had come, made no attempt to stop this acclamation, which would later be celebrated in Christian churches as Palm Sunday. Jesus let the excitement die down, and instead of working miracles, as the priests had expected, he spent the next three days, Monday, Tuesday, and Wednesday, largely in prayer on the Mount of Olives outside the city. Meanwhile, Judas Iscariot, tempted by Satan, went to the priests and asked, "What will ye give me, and I will deliver him unto you? And they covenanted with him for thirty pieces of silver. And from that time he sought opportunity to betray him" (Mt 26:15–16). The best occasion, he decided, was on the Thursday, after supper, when Jesus went to the mount to pray. It would be dark, with no one about, and he would (he said) indicate which was Jesus by kissing him in greeting. The priests, who feared a Jesus mob in the daytime, agreed, and said they would be there with their Temple guards.

The Passover, or feast of unleavened bread in the Jewish calendar, was spread over several days. Thursday was a feast day, followed by a fast (Friday), then the Passover (Saturday). The disciples asked Jesus on Tuesday where he wished to have the feast. He told two of his disciples: "Go ye into the city, and there shall meet you a man bearing a pitcher of water: follow him. And wheresoever he shall go in, say ye to the goodman of the house, The Master saith, Where is the guestchamber, where I shall eat the passover with my disciples? And he will shew you a large upper room furnished and prepared: there make ready for us" (Mk 14:13–15). They obeyed. It was as he said, and on the Thursday evening the Twelve sat down together.

Judas Iscariot was among them, for he needed to identify Jesus to the Temple guards when they came to make the arrest, as arranged, later in the evening. John, who identifies himself in his narrative—"Now there was leaning on Jesus' bosom one of his disciples, whom Jesus loved" (13:23)—quotes Jesus as saying he was "troubled in spirit" and that "one of you shall betray me." Then "the disciples looked one on another, doubting of whom he spake." Peter beckoned to John that he should ask who it should be of whom he spake. He then lying on Jesus' breast saith unto him, Lord, who is it? Jesus answered, He it is, to whom I shall give a sop, when I have dipped it. And when he had dipped the sop, he gave it to Judas Iscariot, the son of Simon. And after the sop Satan entered into him. Then said Jesus unto him, That thou doest, do quickly. Now no man at the table knew for what intent he spake this to him. . . . He then having received the sop went immediately out: and it was night. (13:24–30)

We find it curious that Jesus's warnings against betrayal did not alarm the eleven apostles more: for their lives, too, were at risk. Nor did they take much notice of Jesus's repeated indications that his supreme sacrifice was at hand. It might have been different if women had been present at the Last Supper. They were more sensitive to these hints: to signs and dreams, to sighs and evidence of worry on Jesus's part. But his mother, Mary, and Mary Magdalene, and Martha and Mary of Bethany, and Joanna and Susanna (whose means probably paid the bill for the feast) were not invited. This was an all-male occasion, as often with Passover meals. Jesus wished it so. According to Luke, he began the meal by saying: "With desire I have desired to eat this passover with you before I suffer" (22:15). He also, according to John, wished to perform a last ceremony of humility by washing his apostles' feet (13:4–12). He "laid aside his garments; and took a towel, and girded himself. After that he poureth water into a bason, and began to wash the disciples' feet, and to wipe them with the towel wherewith he was girded." Peter protested.

> JESUS: If I wash thee not, thou hast no part with me.
> PETER: Lord, not my feet only, but also my hands and
>   my head.
> JESUS: He that is washed needeth not save to wash his
>   feet, but is clean every whit: and ye are clean, but not
>   all [meaning Judas].

According to the three synoptics (Mt 26:26–30; Mk 14:22–26; Lk 22:14–20), Jesus used the supper to institute a symbolic ceremony linking the eating of bread and drinking of wine with the coming sacrifice of his body and the shedding of his blood. The words are important and they are almost identical in the three accounts, and parts are repeated in the Acts of the Apostles (2:42–46, 20:7) and Paul's First Epistle to the Corinthians (1:10:16, 11:24–25). Jesus said that the supper was the last meal he would eat before his sacrifice, and the last wine he would drink, "until the kingdom of God shall come" (Lk 22:18). Then Luke describes what followed: "And he took bread, and gave thanks, and brake it, and gave unto them, saying, This is my body, which is given for you: this do in remembrance of me. Likewise also the cup after supper, saying, This cup is the new testament in my blood, which is shed for you." In his letter to the Corinthians, Paul stresses Jesus's command, given by Luke: "This do in remembrance of me."

It is curious that John, who was present, does not record these words by which Jesus instituted the sacrament of Holy Communion, which was placed at the center of the ceremony performed whenever Christians gathered together within two decades of Jesus's death, and has remained such ever since. But John had already recorded Jesus using similar words, calling himself "the bread of life" at the feeding of the five thousand: "I am the living bread . . . the bread that I will give is my flesh, which I will give for the life of the world" (6:51). Moreover, John gives instead a long eschatological address, dealing with death, judgment, hell, and heaven, which Jesus intended as his last serious message to his disciples, and which included some of his most memorable sayings: "Abide in me, and I in you." "I am the vine, ye are the branches." "Let not your heart be troubled: ye believe in God, believe also in me." "In my father's house are many mansions. . . . I go to prepare a place for you." "I am the way, the truth, and the life: no man cometh unto the Father, but by me." "Peace I leave with you, my peace I give unto you." "Greater love hath no man than this, that he lay down his life for his friends." "A little while, and ye shall not see me:

and again, a little while, and ye shall see me: and, Because I go to the Father?" (15:4, 5; 14:1, 2, 6, 27; 15:13; 16:17).

The Last Supper concluded with Jesus leading the eleven apostles in singing a hymn. Not enough attention has been paid to the hymns given in the Gospels. The Magnificat of the Virgin Mary, the Benedictus of Zacharias, the Nunc Dimittis of Simeon, and Gloria in Excelsis sung by the angels (all recorded in Luke) had been complemented by the hosanna hymn, or cry of praise, on Palm Sunday. And it may be that the opening verses of John are a hymn to the Logos originally arranged in three verses. It is a pity we do not have the text of the Last Supper hymn, but it was no doubt one of thanks for the institution of the Holy Communion, for the Acts of the Apostles records the early Christians reflecting the Last Supper tradition, taking communion "with gladness and singleness of heart" and "[p]raising God"—in a way that sounds like hymn singing (2:46–47). And it is fitting that the last hymn recorded in the Gospels shall be a joyful thanksgiving before the horrors to come.

Although the chamber now shown in Jerusalem as the upper room where the Last Supper took place may not be the actual building, the spot is plausible. By contrast, the Mount of Olives and the Garden of Gethsemane are most certainly the places recorded in the Gospels. According to Luke, he warned them yet again of the trouble coming, and when Peter said, "Lord, I am ready to go with thee, both into prison, and to death," Jesus replied sorrowfully, "I tell thee, Peter, the cock shall not crow this day, before that thou shalt thrice deny that thou knowest me." He also warned them that they would need money in the future, and they should sell their goods to buy swords. They replied, "Lord, behold, here are two swords. And he said unto them, It is enough." Then they went into the garden, probably a private one belonging to a wealthy follower, which they were permitted to use. Jesus told them to pray, "And he was withdrawn from them about a stone's cast, and kneeled down, and prayed" (22:31–41).

This long prayer is traditionally called the Agony in the Garden, for in it Jesus both asked for "the cup" to be taken away and submitted to his Father's will—"not my will, but thine, be done." Luke says that "being in an agony he prayed more earnestly: and his sweat was as it were great drops of blood falling down to the ground." An angel appeared, "strengthening him," but how he knew this is not clear, for when Jesus had finished his prayer, "and was come to his disciples, he found them sleeping for sorrow" (22:42–45). Jesus's prayer lasted a long time (Matthew's account says he came back three times to find his apostles asleep). It illustrates the intensity of his communion in prayer with the Father, the enormity of his fear, his horror and revulsion at the prospect of the Crucifixion, and at the same time the courage and resolution with which he put aside his terror and prepared himself for death. Jesus's subsequent calmness during the insults and sufferings he endured is due to the thoroughness with which he prepared himself by prayer—one of the great lessons of his Passion.

Matthew records Jesus coming to his disciples three times (26:40–49). On the third occasion, he said resignedly, "Sleep on now, and take your rest: behold, the hour is at hand." Then the Temple soldiers and the high priest's bodyguards arrived— "a great multitude"—"with swords and staves." Judas, with them, said, "Whomsoever I shall kiss, that same is he: hold him fast." He kissed Jesus, saying, "Hail, master." According to Luke, Jesus replied, "Judas, betrayest thou the Son of man with a kiss?" (22:48). The apostles then became aware of what was happening, and said to Jesus, "Lord, shall we smite with the sword?" (22:49). Luke adds: "And one of them smote the servant of the high priest, and cut off his right ear." Jesus denied them this right to resist: "Suffer ye thus far." He touched the man's ear "and healed him." Then he turned to the priests "and captains of the temple," and said: "Be ye come out, as against a thief, with swords and staves? When I was daily with you in the temple, ye stretched forth no hands against me: but this is your hour, and the power of darkness" (22:50–53).

Then they took him to the high priest's house. In Matthew's account, "all the disciples forsook him, and fled" (26:56). After all their boasting, this was contemptible. One wonders what would have happened if the women had been with them. We cannot see the Virgin Mary abandoning her son, or Mary Magdalene, or the energetic Martha. There would have been a scene of fierce resistance, and blood would have flowed. In justice to the men, Jesus did not call on them to fight, just the contrary. They did not understand his resolve to be meek in suffering, though he had explained it often enough. They were confused. They lacked leadership. Peter did not give it to them. He fled, too. But later he crept back and sat in the outer court of the high priest's palace while Jesus was held within. Three times he was asked, twice by serving maids, once by the mob: "Surely thou also art one of them; for thy speech bewrayeth thee"—a reference to his Galilean accent. He denied it each time ("I know not what thou sayest. . . . I do not know the man"), the third time with curses and swearing. Then the cock crowed, and Peter remembered Jesus's prediction of his betrayal: "And he went out, and wept bitterly" (26:69–75). And what of the real betrayer, the wretched Judas? Matthew says that when he recognized the enormity of what he had done, he "repented himself, and brought again the thirty pieces of silver to the chief priests and elders, Saying I have sinned in that I have betrayed the innocent blood. And they said, What is that to us? see thou to that. And he cast down the pieces of silver in the temple, and departed, and went and hanged himself." Judas and his crime, as well as his dismal fate, gave rise to many stories in the early church. All we know is that "the chief priests took the silver pieces, and said, It is not lawful for to put them into the treasury, because it is the price of blood. And they took counsel, and bought with them the potter's field, to bury strangers in. Wherefore that field was called The field of blood, unto this day" (27:3–8). It was situated on the southern slope of the Valley of Hinnom, near the Kidron Valley, and is known by the Aramaic word Akeldama. Its supposed location, like those of many other places mentioned in the Gospels, is shown to visitors, and those who come to pray for Judas's soul—lost or not, we cannot say—can believe it is the exact spot, if they wish.

Then came the long procedure of Jesus's trials and condemnation, which lasted through the rest of Thursday night, till the cock crowed at dawn, and for most of Friday morning. There were in effect three trials: before the high priest, before Herod Antipas, and before Pilate. All four evangelists contribute something in substance and in detail. What the narratives amount to, in effect and perhaps in intention, is a bitterly ironic condemnation of human justice. Lying and perjury, prejudice and false witness, an eagerness to take innocent life but a determination to avoid any responsibility by passing the decision to others, cowardice on all sides, and not without a vile touch of frivolity—these were the salient characteristics of the trials of Jesus.

The high priest Caiaphas was only too anxious to hustle Jesus off to death, but he was too cowardly to pronounce sentence himself. So he passed the responsibility to Pilate. Pilate was another cowardly and indecisive man. Hearing Jesus was a Galilean, he instantly sent the prisoner off to Herod Antipas: as he said, Herod was the ruler of Galilee and thus had jurisdiction. But Herod, finding Jesus unwilling to plead—he would not recognize the court of the man who had, in his frivolous depravity, decapitated his cousin John the Baptist at the whim of a fan dancer—sent him straight back to Pilate. And Pilate, finally, handed over the responsibility to a mob outside his windows: not a genuine mob of the Jerusalem rabble, either, but a rehearsed and orchestrated one trained in slogan shouting by the priests, their masters. Pilate condemned Jesus not because he was guilty—he, and more important, his wife, believed him innocent—but because he was afraid the Jewish religious leaders would report him to Rome, where his position was shaky. And while these travesties of justice were being enacted, a cluster of servants and soldiers always waited outside for Jesus to be left with them a while, so they could enact a brutal counterpoint to the irresponsible wickedness of their betters by spitting in his face, dressing him up in dirty finery, crowning him with thorns, and sneering at him with obscene slogans. It's hard to say who behaved more badly: those in high places or the underlings who sucked up to them from below.

Jesus, as always, was charitable: "Father, forgive them; for they know not what they do."

Matthew tells us that Jesus was taken to Caiaphas's house, "where the scribes and the elders were assembled" (26:57ff.). John says that Jesus was first brought to the house of Annas, the high priest's father-in-law and predecessor. There, witnesses had been assembled, and Annas asked him about his doctrine. Jesus said, "I spake openly to the world; I ever taught in the synagogue, and in the temple, whither the Jews always resort; and in secret have I said nothing. Why asketh thou me? ask them which heard me, what I have said unto them: behold, they know what I said." At this, one of Annas's officers struck Jesus with the palm of his hand and said, "Answerest thou the high priest so?" Jesus said, "If I have spoken evil, bear witness of the evil: but if well, why smitest thou me?" (18:20–23). Annas decided to have him bound and sent him, escorted, on to Caiaphas, with such witness as he had been able to scrape together. What he, and Caiaphas, wanted was reputable Jews who would swear an oath that Jesus had proclaimed himself the Christ, the King of Israel, and the Son of God, so that, as Matthew says, they could put him to death (26:59). They found "many" to give evidence, but none of the kind they wished. Jesus made no comment, which provoked Caiaphas into saying, "Answerest thou nothing? What is it which these witness against thee?" But as Jesus contrived to "h[o]ld his peace," Caiaphas shouted, "I adjure thee by the living God, that thou tell us whether thou be the Christ, the Son of God!" Jesus replied, "Thou hast said: nevertheless I say unto you, Hereafter shall ye see the Son of man sitting on the right hand of power, and coming in the clouds of heaven" (26:62–64).

This reply was enigmatic, and not what Caiaphas wanted to hear. It was not an admission to shock orthodox Jews, or to persuade the Romans that here was a dangerous rebel. But he decided it would have to do. He declared Jesus had uttered blasphemy and went through the ceremony of rending his garments in disgust. Jewish law listed only a few occasions when garments should be rent, such as death and blasphemy. In the latter case, both the inner and outer garments were torn. But the high priest wore a special double bib which was easy to tear and was expendable, for the law, which had thirty-nine rules, said that in the case of blasphemy the rent had to be the size of a fist and expose the breast, and must never be repaired. So Caiaphas rent both sides of his bib, briefly exposing his skin. Even his rending ceremony had an element of humbug and falseness about it (Mt 26:65; Mk 14:63). But he rent with a will and said: "[W]hat further need have we of witnesses? behold, now ye have heard his blasphemy."

Those present said: "He is guilty of death." Then, says Matthew, "did they spit in his face, and buffeted him; and others smote him with the palms of their hands, Saying Prophesy unto us, thou Christ, Who is he that smote thee?" When the morning came they led Jesus, bound, to the prefectural palace of Pontius Pilate, the governor. According to Luke's account (23:1ff.), "the whole multitude of them" got into the palace, shouting that Jesus had been "perverting the nation," "forbidding [the giving of] tribute to Caesar," "saying that he himself is Christ a King," and "[stirring] up the people." Pilate surveyed the scene with disgust. He had his own information about Jesus's activities and knew the accusations were false. He had been in office for several years and much disliked Jewish religious extremism, having clashed with it twice before. When, to curry favor with his superiors in Rome, he had brought to Jerusalem ensigns bearing Caesar's image, the priests had protested. The Jewish historian Josephus says a large crowd of fanatics held a public fast, which he had broken up by using troops. He had again used troops when the priests and their mob had rioted against his decision to seize Temple funds to pay for a thirty-five-mile aqueduct bringing water to Jerusalem. Many Jews had been killed. There were well-placed Jews living in Rome, and it was not difficult for the priests to make damaging protests to the authorities there. Indeed, six years after the Crucifixion, a similar clash between Pilate's troops and a religious procession, this time a Samaritan one, followed by protest to Rome, led to his dismissal (Josephus, *Jewish Antiquities:* 18.4:1–2).

Pilate was displeased with Caiaphas for bringing a large collection of clamorous militants shouting slogans to his palace. He was also impressed by Jesus's dignified silence. When the hubbub had died down, Pilate asked Jesus, "Art thou the King of the Jews?" Jesus replied, "Thou sayest it" (Lk 23:3). When he spoke at all, that was the line he took throughout: I am accused of all kinds of things but have made no such claims myself—which was the truth. Pilate turned to Caiaphas and said, "I find no fault in this man" (Lk 23:4). He meant: he has done nothing to which the Roman authorities can object. At this the tumult broke out again. "When Pilate heard of Galilee," he seized the opportunity to pass the responsibility to the man who ruled Galilee, Herod Antipas. So he ordered Jesus to be taken to Herod's court, which was in another part of the vast palace originally built by Herod the Great.

Luke says that Herod was "exceeding glad" to see Jesus. He had long wished to do so: he had "heard many things of him" and "hoped to have seen some miracle done by him." He "questioned with him in many words." But Jesus said nothing. He would not speak to the depraved man who had murdered his cousin John at the request of his wife and stepdaughter. While Jesus stood in silence, Caiaphas and his priests kept up their chorus of abuse and accusations. Finally, Herod tired of the game and sent Jesus back to Pilate, but not before his "men of war," as Luke calls them, "mocked him, and arrayed him in a gorgeous robe." Luke, recounting this, says that Pilate's gesture in deferring to Herod's jurisdiction was nonetheless appreciated: "the same day Pilate and Herod were made friends together: for before they were at enmity between themselves" (23:8–12).

So Pilate found himself landed with the problem of Jesus again. He now made a second attempt to spare him. Matthew writes that at the feast of the Passover, it was the governor's practice to release a prisoner at popular request (27:15ff.). Knowing of Jesus's popularity with the local people, he proposed to do this. He assumed the crowd would demand Jesus's freedom, for he knew that the priests had been motivated by "envy" (the word Matthew uses in 27:18) and had little public support. What he did not know was that the priests had organized a demonstration composed of Temple workers, and that this well-schooled mob was outside the palace waiting for the release ceremony; therefore, when Pilate, emboldened by his wife who knew all about Jesus and wanted him released (27:19), sat down on his judgment seat and asked whom he should release, the crowd shouted: "Barabbas." This man, described by Matthew as a "notable" prisoner, was in jail for robbery and murder and for suspicion of planning an insurrection. Normally the priests would have been anxious to have him executed. But they now saw Jesus as a greater danger, so the trained mob had been coached accordingly.

Barabbas was released, to Pilate's disgust. He now asked the crowd, "What shall I do then with Jesus which is called Christ?" They all said unto him: "Let him be crucified." Pilate said, "Why, what evil hath he done?" According to Matthew, "they cried out the more, saying Let him be crucified" (27:22–23).

Pilate then performed a symbolic ceremony of a judge dis-owning himself of responsibility under popular pressure. "[H]e took water, and washed his hands before the multitude, saying, I am innocent of the blood of this just person: see ye to it. Then answered all the people, and said, His blood be on us, and on our children" (27:24–25). Pilate then had Jesus scourged by his soldiers, who used the dreadful *flagellum*, an instrument in which leather thongs weighted with rough pieces of lead or iron were attached to a strong wooden handle. After the scourging, the soldiers who inflicted it "took [him] into the common hall, and gathered unto him the whole band of sol-diers. And they stripped him, and put on him a scarlet robe. And when they had platted a crown of thorns, they put it upon his head, and a reed in his right hand: and they bowed the knee before him, and mocked him, saying, Hail, King of the Jews! And they spit upon him, and took the reed, and smote him on the head" (27:27–30).

Pilate, finding Jesus in this state, made one last attempt to appeal to the pity of the Jewish leaders and the crowd. According to John, he said, "I bring him forth to you, that ye may know that I find no fault in him. Then came Jesus forth, wearing the crown of thorns, and the purple robe. And Pilate saith unto them, Behold the man!" This inspired no remorse or sympathy at all. Led by Caiaphas, the priests and their mob "cried out, saying, Crucify him, crucify him. Pilate saith unto them, Take ye him, and crucify him: for I find no fault in him" (19:4–6). Thus occurred the greatest miscarriage of justice in history, the exemplary and archetypal betrayal of law, of legal procedure, of the rules of evidence and proof, and of all the orderly processes whereby a verdict is reached. Every vice and weakness which vitiates justice was present, from cowardice and perjury to mob rule. Both Jews and Romans, in their different traditions, revered the law. They were the two greatest lawmakers of all time. But here they combined to enact a joint travesty, which has tolled through the centuries as the antithesis of law. It is hard to say who was more to blame for this huge evil: Caiaphas, the accuser, or Pilate, who had the power.

In John's account (19:9–22) the question of power was, indeed, discussed. Pilate, said John, was "afraid" of Caiaphas's accusations, and again examined the scourged and bleeding Jesus, who was wearing his crown of thorns. He asked, "Whence art thou?" But Jesus said nothing. Pilate pressed on: "Speakest thou not unto me? knowest thou not that I have the power to crucify thee, and have power to release thee?" Jesus said, "Thou couldest have no power at all against me, except it were given thee from above: therefore he that delivered me unto thee hath the greater sin." So that was Jesus's own verdict on the relative guilt of Caiaphas and Pilate, Jewish priest and Roman governor. At that point Caiaphas and his crowd said, "If thou let this man go, thou art not Caesar's friend: whosoever maketh himself a king speaketh against Caesar." That was an implied threat to report him to Rome, and Pilate gave way. So he issued the order, from his judgment seat on what was called the Pavement, in Hebrew Gabbatha, for Jesus to be crucified immediately. He also wrote a title, which he commanded to be placed on Jesus's cross: "JESUS OF NAZARETH THE KING OF THE JEWS." It was written, at his direction, in Hebrew and Greek, as well as in Latin. Caiaphas protested, "Write not, The King of the Jews; but that he said, I am King of the Jews." Pilate refused: "What I have written I have written."

Jesus was compelled, according to penal customs, to carry the heavy cross on which he was to be crucified to the place of execution, Golgotha, which meant "the skull." It is not a long distance: you can walk it today, through the narrow streets of old Jerusalem. But Jesus, weak from shock, from loss of blood, having had no sleep and having been subjected to various cruelties, blows, and buffets, stumbled three times under his burden. So the soldiers escorting him compelled a passing stranger, Simon of Cyrene, to help him carry the cross. Luke says that a crowd gathered to watch: not the rehearsed Temple mob but ordinary citizens, "a great company of people, and of women, which also bewailed and lamented him." Jesus stopped in his *via dolorosa* and spoke to them: "Daughters of Jerusalem, weep not for me, but weep for yourselves, and for your children. For, behold, the days are coming, in the which they shall say, Blessed are the barren, and the wombs that never bare, and the paps which never gave suck. Then shall they begin to say to the mountains, Fall on us; and to the hills, Cover us. For if they do these things in a green tree, what shall be done in the dry?" (23:27–31). It is remarkable that Jesus, in his weakness and pain, should have become again the poet, delivering this hymn of warning, which was to be so abundantly justified a generation later in the terrible siege of the city. Many of those weeping women, and more of their children, were to be slaughtered.

In the final stages, indeed, the women took over. Jesus was nailed to the cross, and John, an eyewitness, says, "[T]here stood by the cross of Jesus his mother, and his mother's sister, Mary the wife of Cleophas, and Mary Magdalene." Nothing is said of the male disciples, or the apostles, save one. John himself was there, and Jesus from the cross commended him to his mother: "Woman, behold thy son!" He told John likewise: "Behold thy mother! And from that hour that disciple took her unto his own home" (19:25–27).

There were others present. In Luke's account (23:35ff.), the priests came to deride Jesus, saying, "He saved others; let him save himself, if he be Christ, the chosen of God." The soldiers, too, mocked him, offering him vinegar to drink. Jesus was crucified between two thieves. One, according to Luke,

> railed on him, saying, If thou be Christ, save thyself and us.
> But the other answering rebuked him, saying, Dost not
> thou fear God, seeing thou art in the same condemnation?
> And we indeed justly; for we receive the due reward of
> our deeds: but this man has done nothing amiss. And he
> said unto Jesus, Lord, remember me when thou comest into
> thy kingdom. And Jesus said unto him, Verily I say unto
> thee, To day shalt thou be with me in paradise.

Jesus also spoke as a man, calling on his Father to behold his predicament and give him strength to endure it. His Aramaic words, as recorded by Mark 15:34, were "Eloi, Eloi, lama sabachthani," interpreted as "My God, my God, why hast thou forsaken me?" Some present said, "Behold, he calleth Elias" (Mk 15:35). Jesus also said, "I thirst" (Jn 19:28). He was offered vinegar mixed with water. John, the eyewitness, says that in the afternoon darkness fell. Jesus had been on the cross for three hours. According to Luke, he now cried "with a loud voice" and said, "Father, into thy hands I commend my spirit" (23:46). He is also said to have uttered the phrase "It is finished" (Jn 19:30). Those were his last words, and (according to Luke 23:48 and John 19:30) "he gave up the ghost." His death was edifying, even noble. The centurion commanding the guard

"glorified God, saying, Certainly this was a righteous man."
Other people, says Luke, "smote their breasts" (23:47–48).

The women were with him to the end and helped Joseph of
Arimathaea, who obtained permission from Pilate to take the
body down—after a soldier had certified death by plunging his
spear into Jesus's body, from which issued "blood and water"—
and Nicodemus, who provided spices, to dress and anoint the
corpse and lay it in a tomb. It was hewn out of the rock and
had never been used. So Jesus's body, wrapped in clean linen,
was entombed, and "a great stone" was rolled to the door of the
sepulchre. Mary Magdalene and "the other Mary" were left
"sitting over against the sepulchre" (Mt 27:60–61).

Jesus's three hours on the cross were punctuated by sayings
known from earliest times as "the seven words," and eighteen
hundred years after they were spoken, they were set to incom-
parable music by Joseph Haydn. One was given by Matthew
and Mark conjointly, three by Luke, and three by John. All
embodied love: "Father, forgive them; for they know not what
they do." "Woman, behold thy son. [Son,] behold thy mother."
"To day shalt thou be with me in paradise." "My God, my God,
why hast thou forsaken me?" "I thirst." "It is finished." "Father,
into thy hands I commend my spirit." His suffering, his thirsting,
his triumph seem to sum up his life, which was devoted to expressing his love for humanity. The cross, and the speaking of these
words, mark the conclusion of his sacrificial mission on earth.

IX

† The Resurrection and the Birth of Christianity

ESUS WAS CRUCIFIED, and died, on the Friday. On the third day, Sunday, very early, "when it was yet dark," Mary Magdalene came to the sepulchre. She found the stone had been taken away. She ran back to find Peter and John (who gives this account in chapter 20 of his Gospel) and said, "They have taken away the Lord out of the sepulchre, and we know not where they have laid him." The two apostles went back with her, running. John, being younger, ran faster and got there first. He stooped down, looked in through the low hole into the tomb, and saw the linen clothes scattered about the floor. But he did not dare go in. Peter then arrived and went in. He found the napkin, which had been wrapped about Jesus's head, neatly folded, "in a place by itself." John now went in, too. But neither man yet grasped that Jesus had risen from the dead. They went home, baffled.

But Mary remained, weeping, standing outside the tomb. Then she stooped and looked into it, and saw two angels in white sitting, one at the head and one at the foot of where Jesus had lain. They spoke to her: "Woman, why weepest thou?" She replied, "Because they have taken away my Lord, and I know not where they have laid him." She then turned about and suddenly saw Jesus there. But she did not recognize him. He, too, asked, "Woman, why weepest thou?" She thought he must be the gardener and asked, "Sir, if thou have borne him hence, tell me where thou hast laid him, and I will take him away." He said to her, in tones she recognized, "Mary." She realized it was Jesus and said, "Master."

But he said to her, "Touch me not; for I am not yet ascended to my Father: but go to my brethren, and say unto them, I ascend unto my Father, and your Father; and to my God, and your God." So Mary Magdalene, the former sinner who believed in and worshipped Jesus as God made man, was given the unique privilege of being the first to see the risen Son of God and to announce the Resurrection to the world. She ran back immediately and reported what she had seen, and the words Jesus had spoken to her.

The other three Gospels have little essential to add to this account. Luke confirms that Mary Magdalene was there, but adds that Joanna and Mary the mother of James were also present, as well as "other women." When Peter and the men were told Jesus's body had disappeared, they dismissed the news as "idle tales" and refused to believe the women (24:10). Only when Peter went to the tomb to see for himself did he accept the fact that no body was there. Matthew says that Mary Magdalene "and the other Mary" were greeted at the empty tomb by an angel, whose "countenance was like lightning, and his raiment white as snow." Matthew adds that "for fear of him the keepers did shake, and became as dead men." According to his account, they must have been lying there, immobile and unconscious, when the Marys arrived.

The angel said to the Marys, "Fear not ye: for I know that ye seek Jesus, which was crucified. He is not here: for he is risen, as he said. Come, see the place where the Lord lay. And go quickly, and tell his disciples that he is risen from the dead; and, behold, he goeth before you into Galilee; there shall ye see him: lo, I have told you" (28:1–8). Mark confirms this account, though he says Salome was with the two Marys, and that the angel, described as "a young man . . . clothed in a long white garment" (16:5), spoke to them as in Matthew's account, telling them Jesus had gone ahead into Galilee and that they were to tell Peter. Mark also confirms John's information that Jesus first appeared to Mary Magdalene but that the apostles refused to believe her (16:9–11).

So Sunday morning passed. In the afternoon, two disciples, one called Cleopas, were walking to Emmaus, a two hours' distance from Jerusalem. They already knew about the events of the morning. But when "Jesus himself drew near," they did not recognize him. The account of the meeting is only in Luke, and he may have been told it by Jesus's mother, for it has her poetic touch about it. These three men walked together, and Jesus got the disciples to tell him about recent events—the trial and Crucifixion. They also told him that Jesus's body had disappeared from the tomb. Jesus pointed out that all these happenings had been prophesied, "expound[ing] unto them in all the scriptures the things concerning himself." They still did not recognize him. They arrived at Emmaus, "and he made as though he would have gone further. But they constrained him, saying, Abide with us: for it is toward evening, and the day is far spent." So Jesus stayed with them, and they had supper. He "took bread, and blessed it, and brake, and gave to them." Suddenly, recognizing these familiar gestures, they realized who it was. "[T]heir eyes were opened," says Luke, "and they knew him; and he vanished out of their sight" (24:13–31). The two disciples immediately returned to Jerusalem, "and found the eleven gathered together." They told their story and how they had recognized Jesus when he broke bread. Then, says Luke, "as they thus spake, Jesus himself stood in the midst of them, and saith unto them, Peace be unto you." Luke says they were "terrified" and "supposed that they had seen a spirit." But he pointed out that his body was real and solid: "Behold my hands and my feet, that it is I myself: handle me, and see; for a spirit hath not flesh and bones, as ye see me have." He then showed them the nail holes in his hands and feet. He said he was hungry, too, "[a]nd they gave him a piece of a broiled fish, and of an honeycomb. And he took it, and did eat before them" (24:33–43).

John adds a footnote to this episode, one of those touches of detail which gives such vivid reality to the Gospels. The apostle Thomas was not present when the others saw Jesus eat his broiled fish and honeycomb. He refused to believe what they told him, saying, "Except I shall see in his hands the print of the nails, and put my finger into the print of the nails, and thrust my hand into his side, I will not believe." John says that eight days later, when the disciples, Thomas included this time, were in a room, Jesus appeared, walking through the shut door. He "stood in the midst, and said, Peace be unto you." He said to Thomas, "Reach hither thy finger, and behold my hands; and reach hither thy hand, and thrust it into my side: and be not faithless, but believing." Thomas said, "My Lord and my God." Jesus replied, "Thomas, because thou hast seen me, thou hast believed: blessed are they that have not seen, and yet have believed" (20:24–29).

John records a further appearance, by the Sea of Galilee, to Peter, Thomas, Nathanael, the sons of Zebedee, and two other disciples. They went fishing all night but caught nothing.

When day broke they saw Jesus on the shore and did not recognize him. He said, "Children, have ye any meat?" They
answered, "No." He said, "Cast the net on the right side." They
did, and caught 153 fish. John said to Peter, "It is the Lord."
Jesus had lit a charcoal fire and laid out bread. He invited
them, "Come and dine." He broke the bread and gave it to
them "and fish likewise." This, said John, was "the third time
Jesus shewed himself to his disciples" (21:1–14).

Luke says that Jesus's last act was to lead his disciples out to
Bethany; he then gave them his blessing and was "carried up
into heaven" (24:50–51). Mark gives his final command: "Go
ye into all the world, and preach the gospel to every creature"
(16:15). Matthew adds a detail. He says Jesus told the eleven
apostles to meet him on a mountain in Galilee. When they
assembled together, he said, "All power is given unto me in
heaven and in earth. Go ye therefore, and teach all nations,
baptizing them in the name of the Father, and of the Son, and
of the Holy Ghost." This was the first time the doctrine of the
Trinity was clearly enunciated. He said their teaching was to
include all he had "commanded" them. His last words to them,
before ascending into heaven, were: "I am with you always,
even unto the end of the world" (28:16–20).

We thus come to the end of Jesus's life on earth. I have
followed closely the text of the four Gospels. They are based
primarily on the memories of Jesus's mother, Mary; the evi-

dence of Peter, whom Jesus always treated as the leader of the apostles and confided much in him; on the individual memories of apostles, and their collective memory, the basis of their teaching after Jesus left them; and finally on the account given by John, an eyewitness to many of the events in Jesus's ministry. He was the only one of the apostles not to be martyred, and in his old age he put his memories of Jesus down in writing.

There is a further important source: St. Paul. He was born Saul, in Tarsus, a major city of Cilicia in southeast Asia Minor. The most likely year of his birth was AD 9, so he was about twelve years younger than Jesus. He was born a Roman citizen, of a Hellenized family, and probably spoke fluent Greek and Latin. But he was a circumcised Jew who knew Hebrew and probably Aramaic, Jesus's native tongue. He was well educated, studied under the famous Jewish scholar Gamaliel the Elder in about 20, and was prominent among the orthodox Jews who persecuted the followers of Jesus soon after his ascension into heaven. According to the Acts of the Apostles, an early Christian text compiled by the same Greek doctor who was responsible for the written version of Luke's gospel, Paul was a young man present at the time when Stephen, the first Christian martyr, was stoned to death about one year after Jesus's ascension. He continued to take part in the persecution of Christians until a miraculous event, at the entrance to Damascus, converted him. Thereafter he met all Jesus's surviving friends,

cross-examined them about Jesus's life, teachings, and sayings
and traveled widely with Barnabas. Paul made it his business
to learn everything he could about Jesus and then to convey
it, in systematic form, to the Greek-speaking Gentiles outside
Palestine. He taught in public but he also wrote letters of instruction to the earliest Christian communities, in Corinth,
Rome, and elsewhere, and some of these have survived: the
first Christian documents.

There are two points on which Paul's written evidence is
important. First, he gives an account of Jesus's Resurrection,
which is the first, in written form, to have survived. Paul says
Jesus was seen first by Peter, then by the other apostles. Then
"he was seen of above five hundred brethren at once; of whom
the greater part remain unto this present, but some are fallen
asleep." Then, says Paul, Jesus was seen by James, then by all
the apostles together: "And last of all he was seen of me also,
as of one born out of due time" (1 Cor 15:3–8). Paul's testimony is impressive because his other references to Jesus and
his characteristic qualities and behavior—his personality—
accord remarkably well with the figure presented in the four
Gospels, though Paul cannot have seen any of them in written
form. Moreover, he gives an accurate description of Jesus's
institution of the sacrament of Holy Communion at the Last
Supper, which is worth quoting: "[H]e . . . took bread: And
when he had given thanks, he brake it, and said, Take, eat:

this is my body, which is broken for you: this do in remembrance of me. After the same manner also he took the cup, when he had supped, saying, This cup is the new testament in my blood: this do ye, as oft as ye drink it, in remembrance of me" (1 Cor 11:23–25).

The final confirmatory document is the Acts of the Apostles, compiled by Luke (who was much in the company of Paul). Jesus, commissioning his disciples to spread his message to all the peoples of the earth, had said he would send the Holy Ghost to help, comfort, and inspire them, both physically and spiritually. The promise was fulfilled later in the spring of the same year, at the Jewish feast of Pentecost. It is described in chapter 2 of the Acts. This feast was an event which brought to Jerusalem Jewish pilgrims from all over the Roman Empire and beyond. There were, says Luke, "Parthians, and Medes, and Elamites, and the dwellers in Mesopotamia, and in Judaea, and Cappadocia, in Pontus, and Asia, Phrygia, and Pamphylia, in Egypt, and in the parts of Libya about Cyrene, and strangers of Rome, Jews and proselytes, Cretes and Arabians. . . ."

Jesus's disciples "were all with one accord in one place," the account says, hoping to make converts. But in what language should they speak? Few of the visitors knew Aramaic or spoken Hebrew. Few of the disciples could speak Greek or Latin. "[S]uddenly there came a sound from heaven as of a rushing mighty wind, and it filled all the house where they were sitting. And there appeared unto them cloven tongues like as of fire, and it sat upon each of them. And they were all filled with the Holy Ghost."

When the disciples went outside into the milling crowds of Jews from all nations, they found that the language difficulty had disappeared. The disciples "began to speak with other tongues, as the Spirit gave them utterance." More and more people came to listen, as the word got around—and "every man heard them speak in his own language." Some mocked, saying, "These men are full of new wine." But Peter "lifted up his voice" and said, "[T]hese are not drunken, as ye suppose, seeing it is but the third hour of the day." Peter, not normally a man of poetry, was inspired to speak with strong rhythms that I have set here in verse:

> Saith God, I will pour out of my Spirit, upon all flesh:
> and your sons and your daughters shall prophesy,
> and your young men shall see visions,
> and your old men shall dream dreams:
> And on my servants and on my handmaidens
> I will pour out in those days of my Spirit;
> and they shall prophesy:
> And I will shew wonders in the heavens above,
> and signs in the earth beneath;
> blood, and fire, and vapour of smoke: . . .

> Therefore let all the house of Israel know assuredly,
>
> that God hath made that same Jesus,
>
> whom ye have crucified,
>
> both Lord and Christ. (2:37–41)

This great Pentecostal hymn, heard in different languages, had its effect. They "were pricked in their heart" and asked, "[W]hat shall we do?" Peter replied, "Repent, and be baptized every one of you in the name of Jesus Christ." So they proceeded to the first mass baptism, "about three thousand souls," and the Christian Church was born.

I have tried to tell the story of Jesus of Nazareth, his life, death, Resurrection, and ascent into heaven, as simply and factually as possible. I have used primarily the four Gospel accounts which reached written form not long after the events they described, and which are essentially the memoirs of eyewitnesses to them. I have used throughout the authorized translation into English done in the early seventeenth century, known as the King James Version, because it combines better than any other a high degree of literal accuracy with archaic verbal elements which remind us we are dealing with events of two millennia ago. It is also a work of art.

This is important because the Gospels are literary as well as historical and spiritual documents. Brief, single-minded, direct, and purposeful, they constitute in combination one of the finest works to come down to us from antiquity. This is because they are short biographies, mutually reinforcing and correcting, of a man who was himself a poet and who used words with an astonishing gift for their meaning and resonance and delight. In his imagery and metaphors, in the way he told his stories and parables, in his constant invention of new ways of saying things, he was not merely a superb teacher but a great artist. He also drew people into his discourse and listened to them, asking them questions and commenting on their answers. A high percentage of the Gospels is speech given verbatim, often dialogue. It is vivid: one can hear it. That is one reason why so much of its phraseology has passed into common usage and literary reference in all the tongues of the world. At the beginning of the twenty-first century we still use the language of Jesus and his contemporaries—spoken in Aramaic, then translated into Greek—as often as ever, because it has become part, and a much-loved one, of our own. We hear Jesus for ourselves, almost as though we were sitting at his feet, on the mount. It is part of the continuing miracle of global communication which began on the feast of Pentecost.

The Gospels are designed to be read and reread. The oftener we do so, the greater our delight in them, the deeper our understanding, and the more we grasp their realism. They are the truth. What they tell us actually happened. The characters are real. The details are strangely, sometimes mysteriously, convincing. As we go on reading, the many centuries which intervene gradually slip away, and we become familiar with a world not so different from our own. Palestine in the first century AD was a land crowded (just as our earth is crowded) with a multiracial, multireligious population. The people believed themselves to be civilized, with ancient traditions of law, spiritual life, and government. But their tranquillity was constantly disturbed by barbarous events and acts of savagery. There was a sense of impending catastrophe. Wild visions of a terrifying future were discussed. There were prophets of both doom and utopias.

Government, both spiritual and temporal, was supposedly a blessing, being based, on the one hand, on the Law of Moses and, on the other, on Roman law. There were codes, precedents, courts, parchments—and plenty of lawyers. In practice it was corrupt, mendacious, grossly inefficient, and spasmodically cruel. It did not dispense justice so much as whim. It was run by men who were plainly inadequate and sometimes monsters. Herod the Great was an evil man who murdered innocent children to protect his throne. Herod's son Antipas was a spendthrift hedonist, not unlike some Arabian princes today, but he was also a man who mingled his frivolities with an occasional murder. Caiaphas, the high priest, was an evil man like Herod, with an added dimension of hypocrisy, spiritual pride, and a peculiar malice toward good men. Pontius Pilate was an archetype of the weaknesses with which we are daily familiar in our own political world: a pretense to uphold truth and justice and to heed public opinion, combined with indecision, cowardice, and a final tendency to bow to pressure groups, even when knowing them to be wrong. Every aspect of bad government we experience today finds its counterpart in first-century Palestine, not least the listless mediocrity which was its usual characteristic.

Beneath the rulers were the contrasting worlds of the rich and the poor: men feasted unconcernedly while most did without and a few starved. The Gospels paint this panorama in vivid shades. There was a great deal of charity, institutional and personal; much of it was quite ineffective and hopeless: "The poor always ye have with you." Cripples were ubiquitous. The destitute begged. Pious men took high seats in the synagogue or stood in the streets praying aloud. The Gospels tell it all. They show the activity of the good amid the prevailing indifference: rough men like Peter who were willing to leave their jobs to work, unpaid, with just their keep, for the common cause. And there were the women—the Virgin Mary, Mary Magdalene, Martha, Susanna, Joanna, and many others who were decent and generous, like the widow with her mites, or trusting and long-suffering, like the crone with "an issue of blood." Most of them were poor, a few wealthy; some, like Pilate's wife, superstitious and yearning for spiritual help, we hear of only offstage. We find women in every chapter of the Gospels, almost on every page: the human pulse of emotion, the conduit of love. Their presence compensates for the cruelty, the sneers, the insensitivity, and the roughness we also find on almost every page.

Amid all this teeming humanity is the gregarious, friendly figure of Jesus: always there, teaching, listening, sometimes just chatting at a well or when dining or supping with people of all kinds. Occasionally he was stern. Once or twice he showed righteous anger. But he was usually soft-spoken and genial; images from the fields and groves, or from animal life, were always on his lips. He was a fascinating, irresistible figure, radiating love, benevolent, forgiving, talking always of mercy, smiling often. He was a serious man nonetheless, one who spoke with authority; a man to respect, obey, follow; a man who seemed to, perhaps occasionally really did, emanate light—one of his favorite words—and dispel the dark side of life. He was clearly a man who, despite his meekness, challenged official authority, especially that of those who dealt in spiritual matters. So they had him watched. Always, at his elbow, were agents, spies, informers, and provokers, committing his words to memory so that they could be twisted when used in court. He was a man rarely alone. But when he was solitary, he prayed, kneeling. He prayed often, even on the cross: "Father, forgive them; for they know not what they do."

Jesus lived in a cruel, unthinking world, and his life and death formed an eloquent protest against it. He offered an alternative: not an outward life of revolution and reform but an inner life of humility and love, of generosity and mercy, of forgiveness and hope. We live in a cruel world, too, one just as unthinking, though teeming with knowledge, universities, communications, expertise. So Jesus's alternative is still relevant: "I am the way, the truth, and the life." If Jesus were to appear again today, we can be sure not only that he would find countless followers but equally that he would be persecuted and killed. The Christianity he bequeathed has not been tried and failed. As G. K. Chesterton once wrote, it has been found difficult and left untried. But it remains at our disposal. Its message, at its simplest, is: do as Jesus did. That is why his biography, in our terrifying twenty-first century, is so important. We must study it, and learn.

Further Reading

On the historicity of Jesus, the two most valuable books are E. P. Sanders, *The Historical Figure of Jesus* (London, 1994); and Robert Geis, *The Christ from Death Arisen* (Lanham, Md., 2008). For the Gospels, see Andrew Lincoln, *The Gospel According to St. John* (London, 2005); Ulrich Luz, *Matthew*, 3 vols. (Minneapolis, 1989–2005); John Nolland, *The Gospel of Matthew* (Grand Rapids, 2005); Joel B. Green, *The Gospel of Luke* (Grand Rapids, 1997); Joel Marcus, *Mark 1–8* and *Mark 8–16* (New York, 1999); and John R. Donahue and Daniel J. Harrington, *The Gospel of Mark* (Collegeville, Minn., 2002). Among good recent books are Richard Bauckham, *Jesus and the Eyewitnesses: The Gospels as Eyewitness Testimony* (Grand Rapids, 2006); Gerald O'Collins, *Jesus: A Portrait* (London, 2008); and Pope Benedict XVI, *Jesus of Nazareth* (trans., London, 2007). For background I have used Walter A. Elwell, ed., *Encyclopaedia of the Bible*, 2 vols. (London, 1988); and James Hastings et al., *A Dictionary of Christ and the Gospels*, 2 vols. (Edinburgh, 1906), which, though old, is very full and useful.

Index

Acts of the Apostles, 63, 188, 190, 217, 219–21
adultery, 28, 89, 121
Aeneas, 63
Agony, 43, 84, 105, 190–92
Akeldama, 194
Andrew, Saint, 49–50, 52, 119, 128–29
angels, 16–17, 19, 20–21, 132, 190, 212
Anna, 25
Annas, 151, 196
Annunciation, 16–17
anointing, 131, 138–39, 184–85
Antioch, 2
Antonia fortress, 14, 181
Antony, Mark, 14
"apostolic succession," 53
Aramaic language, 1, 15, 19, 28–29, 52, 64–65, 72, 194, 205, 217, 219, 222
Archelaus, 22–23
Aristotle, 12, 91
art and architecture, 2, 22, 45–46, 51
Ascension, 212, 217

astrology, 21
Augustine, Saint, 114–15
Augustus, emperor of Rome, 13, 20

baptism, 27, 38–42, 119, 121, 128, 221
Barabbas, 200
Barnabas, 218
Bartholomew, Saint, 52 59
Beatitudes, 86, 87, 100
Beelzebub, 68
Benedictus, 100, 190
Bethany, 73–75, 141, 183–85, 187, 216
Bethesda, 132–33, 150
Bethlehem, 20–23
Bethsaida, 66
Bible, 5, 221
    see also New Testament; Old Testament
blasphemy, 151, 196–98
blindness, 66–67, 102, 133–34
bread, 14, 64, 119–20, 130, 138, 140, 180, 188–89, 214, 216, 218–19

Caesar, Julius, 12, 179
Caesarea, 13, 81
Caiaphas, 76, 121, 150–51, 180,
     192–98, 199, 202–3, 223–24
Calvary, 23
Cana, wedding at, 59–61, 64, 121
Canaanites, 140, 148
Capernaum, 48–50, 65, 68–69, 81,
     148
Caravaggio, 22, 51
Carlyle, Thomas, 120–21
catacombs, 146
celibacy, 143–44
census, 20, 159
centurions, 65, 66, 205–6
charity, 15, 87, 91–93, 108–12,
     117–18, 134, 150, 224
Chesterton, G. K., 226
children, 70, 84, 102, 104–5,
     144–50, 151, 174
Christianity:
   art and architecture of, 2, 22,
     45–46, 51
   conversion to, 75, 114–15, 149
   growth of, 2, 92, 152, 216,
     220–21, 226
   historical evaluation of, 1–5,
     152, 161–63, 173–74, 226
   influence of, 2–3, 152, 161–63
   Judaism compared with, 38, 107,
     141–42
   moral values of, 3, 23, 38, 62–63,
     76, 83, 141, 173
   origins of, 2, 151, 170, 220–21
   persecution of, 24, 129, 217
   prayer in, 82–86
   priesthood of, 52–53, 143–44

   reformation of, 38, 161, 170
   social impact of, 170, 172,
     173– 74
   women in, 143–44, 146
circumcision, 23, 217
Cleophas, 204, 213–14
commandments, 51, 90–91, 157–74
Communion, 41, 187–90, 218–19
constitutional arrangements,
     172
Contarelli Chapel, 51
conversions, religious, 75, 114–15,
     149
Corinthians, Epistles to the, 1, 189,
     218–19
cripples, 67–68, 69, 121, 132–33,
     150, 224
cross, 50, 129, 131, 173, 203–6
crown of thorns, 201–2
Crucifixion, 23, 41, 81, 92, 105,
     122, 129, 131, 138, 172, 173,
     174, 179, 181, 182–83, 185,
     191–92, 198, 201, 202, 203–6,
     213, 214, 225–26
Cyrenius, 20

Damascus, 51, 217
Darwin, Charles, 3, 44–45
David, 15, 16, 20, 38, 158, 181
dead, raising of the, 63–64, 70–76,
     121, 148, 183–84
Dead Sea Scrolls, 30
Decalogue, 92
Decapolis, 64, 81
Deuteronomy, Book of, 90–91
devils, 63, 68, 69–70, 75, 120, 138,
     145

divorce, 142
dogma, religious, 12, 29, 83, 135,
   140–43, 169–70, 223
Dorcas, 63–64
Doria Pamphilj Gallery, 22
"Doubting Thomas," 52, 215

Ecclesiasticus, Book of, 167–68
economic issues, 15, 62, 86–88,
   109–18, 134, 141, 145–46, 149,
   159–60, 174, 185, 224
Egypt, 11, 22–23, 219
elders, 150–51, 165, 196, 217
Elias, 48
Eliseus, 48
Elizabeth, 17–19, 23, 38, 100
Emmaus, 213–14
Enlightenment, 161, 170
Epistles of St. Paul, 1, 188, 189,
   218–19
equality, 165–66
Essenes, 30, 38
Euripides, 29
evangelists, 63, 127–28, 166, 172,
   194, 206
evil, 3–4, 23, 43–45, 62, 67–68, 89,
   131, 161, 224
exorcisms, 62, 69–70

faith, 47, 65–66, 70–71, 131–35,
   139–40, 147–48
families, 26, 30, 142, 144–45,
   162
feet-washing, 138–39, 187–88
fishermen, 48–50, 51, 59, 61, 82
forgiveness, 139, 195–96, 225–26
free will, 162–64

Gabbatha, 203
Gabriel, 16–17
Galilee, 15, 23, 41–42, 47, 61, 63,
   81, 109, 135, 193, 213
Gamaliel the Elder, 217
Garden of Gethsemane, 43, 84,
   105, 190–92
Gaul, 12
Gaza, 23
Gentiles, 25, 62–63, 66, 91–93,
   217, 218, 219
Gergesa, 69–70
Gloria in Excelsis, 190
God:
   as creator, 152, 171–72
   as Father, 3, 27, 43, 83–85, 90,
      92–93, 112, 136, 144–45, 152,
      158, 191, 205, 212, 225–26
   Jesus as Son of, 3, 16–18, 27, 30,
      40–41, 43, 59, 73, 75, 83–84,
      92, 112, 130–31, 136, 144–45,
      152, 158, 191, 196–97, 204,
      212
   justice of, 165–66
   Kingdom of, 44–45, 83, 90, 91,
      92–93, 104, 106, 114–15, 130,
      134, 147, 148, 149, 151,
      157–60, 163
   love of, 164–67
   mercy of, 110–14, 167–69
   as omniscient and omnipresent,
      4, 40–41, 118–19, 171
   tripartite nature of, 4, 27, 43
   will of, 43, 84–85, 136, 144,
      191
   worship of, 45, 82–86, 116, 136,
      162

God (*cont.*)
  as Yahweh, 83, 118–19
Golgotha, 203
Good Samaritan, 108–12, 164
Good Shepherd, 31, 103
Gospels, 5, 15–19, 27–28, 31,
    39–47, 52, 63, 72–73, 82–83,
    86, 100, 105, 108, 118, 127–28,
    143–44, 146, 149, 151, 160,
    162, 165, 166–67, 168, 169,
    179, 188–90, 194, 215, 216–17,
    218, 220–22, 224, 225
  see also specific gospels
government, 223–24
grace, 167–69
Great Commandment, 90–91,
    164–65
Greece, 11, 12, 14
Greek language and literature, 1,
    28, 29, 62–63, 91, 142, 203,
    217, 218, 219, 222

Haydn, Joseph, 206
healing of sick, 63, 64–68, 70–71,
    131–33, 148–49, 150, 180,
    224
Hebrew language and literature,
    15, 28–29, 203, 217, 219
Hebrews, 135, 157
heresy, 114–15
Herod Antipas, 41–42, 121,
    131–32, 145, 159, 174, 180,
    194, 199–200, 223
Herodias, 42, 183
Herod the Great, 13–14, 20,
    21–22, 24, 26, 86, 199, 223
hierarchies, social, 165–66

high priests, 37, 38, 40, 41–42,
    47–48, 75–76, 83, 108, 115,
    150–51, 180–83, 185, 192–98,
    199
Hillel, 142
Hinnom Valley, 194
Holy Family, 26, 30, 144–45
Holy Spirit, 3, 16, 17, 19, 27, 40, 42,
    43, 82, 136, 219–20
Homer, 29
Horace, 13

idolatry, 44–45
innocence, 22–23, 42, 147–48,
    150, 194–98, 223
Iran, 181
Isaiah, Book of, 39, 47–48
Israel, 25, 65, 140

Jacob, 16, 135
Jairus, 70–72, 148
James, Saint, 49, 52, 71, 129,
    151–52
James, Saint (son of Alphaeus), 52
Jericho, 108
Jerusalem, 13–14, 17, 73, 81, 110,
    180–81, 182, 183, 184–85,
    198, 203–4, 214, 219
Jesus Christ:
  Agony of, 43, 84, 105, 190–92
  anointing of, 131, 138–39, 184–85
  apostles of, 43–44, 46, 47–53, 59,
    61, 71, 73, 86, 92, 105, 106,
    119–20, 127–30, 143, 145, 149,
    151–52, 158, 173, 186–90,
    204, 212–22; *see also specific
    apostles*

Index

arrest of, 81, 174, 182–83, 185–87, 192–93

artistic images of, 2, 45–46, 51

Ascension of, 212, 217

authority of, 46–47, 51, 119, 180–81, 225

baptism of, 27, 38–42, 119, 121, 128

Bethlehem as birthplace of, 20–22

betrayal of, 185–87, 192, 193–94

biographies of, 1–6, 162, 222, 226

birth of, 11, 14, 20–23, 27, 31, 83, 100, 150

blasphemy charge against, 151, 196–98

body of, 131, 206

as carpenter, 30

childhood of, 25–28, 31

children favored by, 70, 146–50, 174

circumcision of, 23

commandments of, 51, 90–91, 157–74

compassion of, 64–65, 91–93, 109, 111–12, 127–52, 168, 174

cross of, 50, 129, 131, 173, 203–6

crowds attracted by, 64, 68–69, 72, 127–28, 158–59, 180–81, 185

crown of thorns of, 201–2

Crucifixion of, 23, 41, 81, 92, 105, 122, 129, 131, 138, 163, 172, 173, 174, 179, 181, 182–83, 185, 191–92, 198,

201, 202, 203–6, 213, 214, 225–26

dead raised by, 63–64, 70–76, 121, 148, 183–84

death of, 204–6

death sentence for, 183, 198–204

as descendent of David, 15, 16, 20, 21

divine nature of, 3–5, 43, 46–47, 82, 121, 134, 151–52, 173, 174, 211–16

dogma opposed by, 12, 29, 83, 135, 140–43, 169–70, 223

economic and social issues as viewed by, 109–18, 141, 145–46, 159–60

education of, 26–30

elderly respected by, 150–51

enemies of, 50–53, 67–69, 72, 75–76, 132–33, 143, 149, 157–62, 180–83, 192–204, 225

epiphany of, 151–52

existence of, 4

exorcisms by, 63, 69–70

faith in, 47, 65–66, 70–71, 131–35, 139–40, 147–48

family of, 26, 30, 144–45

feet-washing by, 187–88

fishermen summoned by, 48–50, 51, 59, 61, 82

forgiveness by, 139, 168, 195–96, 225–26

gaze of, 46–47, 51, 128

Gentile followers of, 25–26, 62–63, 66, 91, 217, 218, 219

as Good Shepherd, 31, 103

Index

Jesus (*cont.*)
  high places visited by, 31, 44–45,
    52–53, 151–52
  humanism of, 84–85, 88–93,
    127–52, 164–66
  human nature of, 1–2, 3, 5, 47
  imagery used by, 14–15, 29–30,
    103–5, 112, 117, 130, 131, 170,
    222
  imitation of, 47, 160–62
  immaculate conception of,
    15–19, 27
  Incarnation of, 92, 142
  Jerusalem entered by, 184, 185
  as Jew, 23, 27–29, 135
  Jewish followers of, 62–63,
    73–76, 108–10, 130–31, 217
  Kingdom of God described by,
    44–45, 83, 90, 91, 92–93, 104,
    106, 114–15, 130, 134, 147,
    148, 149, 151, 157–60, 163
  as king of the Jews, 21–26, 38,
    75, 157–58, 180–81, 196, 198,
    199, 201, 203
  as Lamb of God, 49
  Last Supper of, 41, 130, 187–90,
    218–19
  light-and-darkness imagery of,
    103–5, 112, 117, 131, 170
  as Logos, 104–5, 190
  love preached by, 88–93, 99,
    147–48, 164–67
  menial work done by, 30–31
  as Messiah, 49, 136, 157–58
  metaphors and similes used by,
    99–105, 112, 133–34, 137–38,
    159–60, 163, 222

ministry or mission of, 19, 30–31,
    37, 42, 46–53, 62, 70, 73,
    99–122, 141–42, 166–67, 172,
    181, 216–17
  miracles of, 37, 39, 44, 48–49,
    59–76, 121, 130, 131–33,
    148–49, 180–84, 199
  missing years of, 27–31
  name of, 16, 19
  natural phenomenon altered by,
    63, 82, 85, 152, 170–71
  Nazareth as residence of, 15, 23,
    26, 27–30
  parables of, 29–30, 81–82, 86,
    88, 90, 99–122, 141, 165, 204
  Passion of, 84, 184, 192–206
  personality of, 5, 29–31, 42–43,
    46–47, 51, 114–15, 127–52,
    162, 168–69, 218, 225
  physical appearance of, 2, 45–47,
    51, 128, 151–52
  praying by, 30, 42–43, 82–86, 89,
    185–86, 190–92, 224, 225–26
  prophesies about, 16–17, 24–25,
    39, 42, 214
  as prophet, 136, 139
  questions asked by, 118–20
  religious authority questioned
    by, 41–42, 47, 53, 67–68, 69,
    72, 75–76, 83, 132–33, 136,
    137–38, 149, 150–51, 157–60,
    165, 168–71, 180–83, 192–98,
    199, 201–2, 217
  Resurrection of, 2, 64, 105, 120,
    172, 206, 211–16, 218, 221
  as revolutionary, 83, 157–62, 172–
    73, 180–81, 182, 196–98, 226

236

Index

robe given to, 201–2

sacrifice of, 84, 158, 173, 182–83, 188–92, 206

salvation offered by, 65–66

as Savior and Redeemer, 21, 23, 24–26, 39–41, 49, 65–66, 74, 92, 110–11, 130–31, 136, 137, 157–58

sayings of, 88, 90, 122, 205, 206

Scourging of, 121, 197–98, 201, 202

"seven last words" of, 122, 205, 206

sick healed by, 63, 64–68, 131–33, 148–49, 150, 180, 224

signs given by, 62–63, 65, 72

silences of, 86, 120–22, 168, 199

sins absolved by, 39–41, 110–11, 157–58

sociability of, 114–15, 127–52, 168–69

as Son of God, 3, 16–18, 27, 30, 40–41, 43, 59, 73, 75, 83–84, 92, 112, 130–31, 136, 144–45, 152, 158, 191, 196–97, 204, 212

as Son of Man, 67, 120, 138, 192, 197

spear wound of, 206

teachings of, 1–5, 14–15, 19, 29–30, 38, 46–48, 62–63, 64, 76, 81–93, 99–122, 130–31, 140–43, 157–74, 180–81, 182, 216–18, 225–26

tomb of, 131, 206, 211–12

Transfiguration of, 43, 151–52

travels of, 81–82, 145

trials of, 194–98, 214

truths espoused by, 46–47, 62–63, 104–5, 136, 159, 170–71, 182, 222–23, 224, 226

universalism of, 91–93, 109, 111–12, 164–65

in wilderness, 42–45, 59, 121

wisdom of, 25–27

witnesses against, 194, 196–97

women as followers of, 134–46, 150, 187, 192–93, 203–4, 206, 212–13, 224–25

Jewish Antiquities (Josephus), 198

Jews:

culture of, 14–15, 87

education of, 15, 16, 26–30

feast days of, 26, 183, 186, 187–90, 200, 219

as followers of Jesus, 62–63, 73–76, 108–10, 130–31, 217

Gentiles compared with, 25–26, 62–63, 66, 91–93, 217, 218, 219

Jesus as king of, 21–26, 38, 75, 157–58, 180–81, 196, 198, 199, 201, 203

orthodox, 53, 67, 129–33, 136, 137–38, 150–51, 180, 197, 217

political leadership of, 83, 157–62, 180–83, 194–203

see also Judaism

Joanna, 145, 187, 212, 224

Job, Book of, 29, 118–19

John, Gospel of, 3, 29–30, 39–40, 47, 49, 59–60, 72, 73, 74–75, 76, 84, 85, 87, 92, 93, 101, 102, 103, 104–5, 107, 119–20, 121,

John, Gospel of (*cont.*)
   128, 130, 131, 132, 133–34,
   137, 141, 170, 184, 185,
   186–88, 189, 190, 202–3, 204,
   205, 206, 211, 213, 215, 216
John, Saint, 49, 50, 52, 71, 129,
   151–52, 211, 217
John the Baptist, Saint, 17, 23, 27,
   38–42, 45, 49–51, 121, 138,
   183, 194, 199
Jordan River, 39, 42
Joseph, 14, 19–23, 26–27, 30, 48,
   142
Joseph of Arimathaea, 131, 206
Josephus, 5, 198
Judaea, 22, 51, 81, 109, 135, 146,
   180–82, 219
Judah, 17
Judaism:
   authority of, 41–42, 47, 53, 67–68,
     69, 72, 75–76, 83, 132–33,
     136, 137–38, 149, 150–51,
     157–60, 165, 168–71, 180–83,
     192–98, 199, 201–2, 217
   Christianity compared with, 38,
     107, 141–42
   commentaries on, 106, 107
   elders of, 150–51, 165, 196, 217
   laws of, 23–24, 37–38, 83, 91–92,
     107, 134, 140–43, 197, 202,
     223
   moral values of, 15, 37–38, 87
   Mosaic, 141–42, 223
   reformation of, 37–38
   teachings of, 15, 37–38, 87,
     145–46, 157
   see also Jews

Judas Iscariot, 52, 120, 141,
   185–87, 192, 193–94
Jude, Saint, 52
justice, 112, 165–66, 194–98
Justin Martyr, 20

King James Version, 5, 221

Lamb of God, 49
Laocoön and His Sons, 13
Last Supper, 41, 130, 187–90,
   218–19
Latin language and literature,
   12–13, 28, 201, 203, 217, 219
Lazarus (beggar), 62, 108, 110
Lazarus, resurrection of, 64, 72–76,
   183–85
legalism, 12, 29, 83, 135, 140–43,
   169–70, 223
Levites, 40, 108
Leviticus, Book of, 90–91
Livy, 13
loaves and fishes, miracle of, 64, 180
Logos, 104–5, 190
Lord's Prayer, 84
love, 88–93, 99, 147–48, 164–67
Luke, Gospel of, 16, 17, 18, 20–21,
   23–27, 39, 40, 42, 43, 47, 48,
   52, 62, 66, 71, 72, 84, 86, 87–88,
   90, 91, 100, 102, 103, 107–8,
   110–11, 112, 114, 115, 116, 127,
   137–38, 140, 141, 143, 144, 145,
   148–49, 152, 159, 169–70, 173,
   184, 187, 188, 189, 190, 191,
   192, 199–200, 203, 204–5,
   206, 212, 214, 215, 217, 219
Luke, Saint, 15–16

Index

Maccabees, 38
Magnificat, 19, 100, 190
Mark, Gospel of, 39, 42, 47, 50, 51,
  52–53, 63, 67–68, 70, 71–72,
  90, 91, 92, 102, 106, 107, 111,
  115, 117–18, 119, 129, 147, 148,
  149, 152, 164, 171, 186, 188,
  197, 205, 206, 213
marriage, 136, 137, 142, 144–45
Martha, 73–75, 141, 145, 183–85,
  187, 193, 224
martyrs, 24, 129, 217
Mary, Virgin, 15–27, 30, 59–61,
  142, 145, 190, 193, 204, 214,
  216, 224
Mary (mother of James), 212
Mary (sister of Lazarus), 73–75,
  141–42, 183–85, 187
Mary (wife of Cleophas), 204, 206
Mary Magdalene, 120, 145, 193,
  204, 206, 211–12, 224
Massacre of the Innocents, 22, 42,
  223
Matthew, Gospel of, 19, 20, 22,
  39, 40, 41, 42, 43, 44, 47, 50,
  52, 63, 66, 67, 69–70, 71, 86,
  87, 88–89, 90, 92, 100, 101,
  102, 103, 107, 108, 116–17,
  121, 129–30, 140, 142, 144,
  146, 147, 148, 149–50, 152,
  159–60, 165, 171, 173, 185,
  188, 191, 192, 193, 194, 196–97,
  200, 201, 202, 206, 213
Matthew, Saint, 51, 52, 70, 129
mercy, 110–14, 167–69
Messiah, 49, 136, 157–58
miracles, 37, 39, 44, 48–49, 59–76,

  121, 130, 131–33, 148–49,
  180–84, 199
monks, 143–44
monotheism, 37–38
Moses, 38, 83, 86, 133, 141–42, 223
Mount of Olives, 43, 73, 185, 190
murder, 88–89
mustard seed, parable of, 119

Nain, 148
Nathanael (son of Zebedee),
  215–16
Nativity, 20–23
natural phenomenon, 63, 82, 85,
  152, 170–71
Nazareth, 15, 19, 66
Near East, 83, 88, 105–6, 134, 138,
  142, 219
neighborliness, 90–92, 109,
  164–65
New Commandments, 162–74
New Order, 39
New Testament, 18, 38, 41, 60,
  105, 111, 121, 128, 137, 140,
  151
Nicodemus, 130–31, 206
Nunc Dimittis, 100, 190
nuns, 143–44

Old Testament, 16, 28–29, 39, 62,
  88, 90–91, 106, 118–19, 168
  see also specific books
Origen, 24
Ovid, 13

Palestine, 13–14, 52, 109–10, 149,
  158–60, 180–81, 223

Index

Palm Sunday, 185, 190
parables, 29–30, 81–82, 86, 88, 90,
    99–122, 141, 165, 204
Parthenon, 12
Passion, 84, 184, 192–206
Passion Week, 184
Passover, 26, 183, 186, 187–90,
    200
Patras, 129
Paul, Saint, 1, 62–63, 163, 188,
    189, 217–19
Pentecost, 219–21, 222
Peter, Saint, 46, 48–49, 52, 61, 63,
    71, 128–29, 141, 151–52,
    186–87, 188, 190–91, 193,
    211, 212–13, 215–17, 218, 220,
    221, 224
Pharisees, 41–42, 67–68, 69, 75,
    76, 116, 129–30, 138–39, 158,
    159–60, 168–69
Philip, Saint, 52, 119
Philippi, 81
Philip the Tetrarch, 51
piety, 91–92
Pilate, Pontius, 146, 159, 174, 180,
    194, 195, 197, 198–203,
    223–24
Pliny, 5
poetry, 99–101, 141, 204
political issues, 83, 109–18, 141,
    145–46, 157–62, 170, 172, 174,
    180–83, 194–203
Pompey, 11
poverty, 15, 87, 110–11, 114, 134,
    149, 174, 185, 224
power, exercise of, 172
Praetorian Guard, 13

prayer, 30, 42–43, 82–86, 89,
    185–86, 190–92, 224, 225–26
priesthood, 52–53, 143–44
prodigal son, parable of, 112–14
prophets, 39, 48, 136, 139
prostitutes, 146, 150
Psalms, Book of, 29
publicans, 51, 129–30, 138, 150

rabbis, 106
rebirth, spiritual, 147, 151–52
Redeemer, 21, 23, 24–26, 39–41,
    49, 65–66, 74, 92, 110–11,
    130–31, 136, 137, 157–58
Reformation, 38, 161, 170
Renaissance, 161, 170
repentance, 110–14, 130, 139–40,
    221
Rights of Man, 167
Roman Empire, 11–14, 20, 23, 37,
    38, 41–42, 65, 75, 83, 86–87,
    91, 110, 142, 146, 152, 158–60,
    179, 180–81, 194, 203, 205–6,
    217, 219, 223, 298

Sabbath, 49, 63–64, 132–33, 184
sacraments, 41
sacrifices, 84, 89, 102, 110, 158,
    166–67, 173, 182–83, 188–92,
    206
Sadducees, 41–42, 157, 168–69
Salome, 42, 183
Samaritans, 13, 23, 73, 81, 91,
    108–12, 135–37, 139, 157,
    174, 198
Sanhedrin, 131
Sartor Resartus (Carlyle), 120–21

Index

Satan, 42–45, 104, 181, 184, 185
Savior, 21, 23, 24–26, 39–41, 49,
    65–66, 74, 92, 110–11,
    130–31, 136, 137, 157–58
science, 3, 44–45, 170
Scourging, 121, 197–98, 201, 202
scribes, 28, 38, 47, 76, 83, 91, 115,
    168–69, 196
Sea of Galilee, 48–50, 51, 59, 70,
    182, 215–16
sects, religious, 30, 38, 158
Sejanus, 13
self-transformation, 84–85
Seneca, 13
Sermon on the Mount, 86
Sermon on the Plain, 86
"seven last words," 122, 205, 206
sheep, 49, 103, 107, 149
Sidon, 81, 140
signs, 62–63, 65, 72
silence, 86, 120–22, 168, 199
silver, thirty pieces of, 185,
    193–94
silver coin, parable of, 110–11,
    112
Simeon, 24–25, 100, 150, 190
Simon of Cyrene, 203
Simon the Pharisee, 138–40,
    184–85
Simon the Zealot, 52
slavery, 12, 91
social issues, 109–18, 141, 145–46,
    159–60, 170, 172, 173–74
Solomon, 103
Son of God, 3–4, 16–18, 27, 30,
    40–41, 43, 59, 73, 75, 83–84,
    92, 112, 130–31, 136, 144–45,

152, 158, 191, 196–97, 204,
    212
Son of Man, 67, 120, 138, 192, 197
"Sons of Thunder," 52, 129
spikenard, 141, 184–85
star of the East, 20–21
Stephen, Saint, 217
stoning, 28, 73, 183, 217
Suetonius, 5
Summa theologica (Aquinas), 63
Susanna, 145, 187, 224
Sychar, 135–37
synagogues, 47–48, 49, 61, 64,
    67–68, 70, 82, 127, 145–46,
    150–51, 165, 196, 224
synthetic parallelism, 100
Syria, 20, 159, 181

Tacitus, 4
talents, parable of, 117–18
Tarsus, 217
tax collectors, 20, 51, 129, 159
Temple, 13, 14, 17, 24–27, 73, 100,
    110, 134, 145–46, 149, 150–51,
    158–60, 183, 186, 192, 196,
    200, 203
Ten Commandments, 162
Thaddaeus, 52
Thomas, Saint, 52, 73, 215–16
Thomas Aquinas, Saint, 63,
    163
Tiberius, Emperor of Rome, 13, 83,
    159–60, 198, 203
Torah, 16
Transfiguration, 43, 151–52
Trinity, 4, 27, 43
Tyre, 81, 140

Universal Declaration of Human
    Rights, 167
universalism, 91–93, 109, 111–12,
    164–65

vineyard, parable of, 107, 108
Virgil, 13, 29
virginity, 15–19, 116–17
virgins, foolish and wise, 116–17

wealth, 62, 86–88, 110–11, 114, 224
widow's mite, 111, 134, 150, 165,
    224

wine, 59–61, 64, 121, 138,
    188–89
Wise Men, 21–22, 23
women, 134–46, 150, 187,
    192–93, 203–4, 206, 212–13,
    224–25

Yahweh, 83, 118–19

Zacharias, 17, 42, 150, 190
zealotry, 30, 38
Zealots, 38, 158
Zebedee, 49, 50

Say "yes!" to the exciting offer for Disney storybooks!

Dear Parent:

For over 30 years, millions of children and their families have shared the reading fun and family excitement of membership in DISNEY'S WONDERFUL WORLD OF READING®.

Now you're invited to experience the unforgettable fun of sharing eight Disney storybooks -- just like this book you're holding in your hands -- with your child for just $3.99*. Plus, you'll also receive a FREE bonus, a colorful, roomy backpack featuring Winnie the Pooh!

The choice is yours, of course. Just remember: if you're not completely thrilled with your Disney storybooks, you may return them -- at Scholastic's expense -- within seven days with no obligation. The FREE backpack is yours to keep no matter what you decide.

Go ahead, see for yourself. Detach one of the postage-paid reply cards now, while it is on your mind. Take it home, fill it out and drop it in the mail today.

Sincerely,

Emily Reid

Emily Reid
Membership Director

If all the reply cards are gone, write to:

SCHOLASTIC
P.O. BOX 6038
JEFFERSON CITY, MO 65102-6038

Koda

Kenai

Kenai

Denahi

Sitka

Rutt   Tuke

SCHOLASTIC INC.

New York   Toronto   London   Auckland   Sydney
Mexico City   New Delhi   Hong Kong   Buenos Aires

*Long ago, there lived three
brothers who were taught that the
lights of the northern sky were
the spirits of their ancestors.
These spirits had the power
to make changes—small
things into big, winter
into spring, and boys
into men. . . .*

One day, the villagers gathered for a special ceremony. Tanana, the shaman woman, presented Kenai, the youngest of the three brothers, with his totem—the animal symbol he was to follow to become a man.

"Your totem is love," said Tanana, giving him a carved bear totem. "Let love guide your actions, and one day, you will place your mark next to those of our ancestors," she added, pointing to a wall covered with handprints.

"The bear of love?" Kenai frowned. "Wanna trade?" he asked his brothers.

His older brothers laughed. They had
already received their totems. Sitka's was the
eagle of guidance and Denahi's was the wolf
of wisdom.

After the ceremony, the brothers left to
get the fish they had caught for the evening's
feast. "A bear doesn't love anyone," Kenai
said unhappily to Sitka. "They don't think,
they don't feel, they're—"

Just then Denahi found the remains of
the basket that had held their fish. "Thieves!"
shouted Kenai, staring at the bear tracks.

Kenai followed the tracks into the woods to find the basket.

When Kenai didn't return, Sitka and Denahi went after him. It wasn't long before they heard Kenai cry out. He had slipped off a ledge trying to escape from a bear!

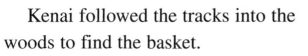

Quickly Denahi distracted the bear while Sitka helped Kenai. But then Denahi slipped into a dangerous crevice. While Kenai helped him, Sitka faced the bear.

Suddenly the bear turned and headed for Kenai and Denahi. To save his brothers, Sitka raised his spear and thrust it down into a crack in the ice. The ice split, and the piece on which Sitka and the bear were standing plunged into the freezing water below.

From far above, Kenai and Denahi saw the bear emerge from the water—but not Sitka. Their oldest brother would now be joining the Great Spirits in the form of his totem—the eagle. Denahi felt great sadness. But Kenai felt great anger!

The next day, Kenai was determined to go after the bear that had caused Sitka's death. But Denahi would not go with him. Angry, Kenai threw his bear totem into a fire and left the village.

Tanana pulled the totem from the fire.

"I've got to go after him," Denahi said, taking the bear totem.

Kenai tracked and eventually found the bear. After a fierce struggle, Kenai fell to the ground. The animal charged towards him. Kenai raised his spear. The bear crashed into him, let out a roar, and then fell silent.

Suddenly lights burst down from the sky and swirled around Kenai. A giant eagle landed next to him and turned into Sitka. Then Kenai felt himself being lifted into the air. He didn't realize that he was being magically transformed into the creature he hated most—a bear!

The lights disappeared and it began to rain.

Just then Denahi arrived and saw a grizzly bear standing on Kenai's clothes. Denahi didn't know Kenai was now a bear. So he thought that the bear had killed Kenai. Before he could react, a bolt of lightning sent the bear tumbling into the river below. Kenai was swept away.

Now it was Denahi's turn to want revenge. He tied Kenai's bear totem to his spear and began to track the bear.

When Kenai opened his eyes the next
morning, Tanana was leaning over him.

Kenai spoke to her excitedly, telling her
all that had happened to him. But all Tanana
could hear were growls.

"Kenai, I don't speak bear!" said the
wise woman.

Kenai didn't understand. Then he looked into the river at his reflection. "No!" he shouted. He twisted around and looked at his furry tail. "AAAHHH!" he cried.

To get Kenai's attention, Tanana took off her boot and bonked him on the head with it. "Listen to me! Sitka did this!" said Tanana. "Take it up with your brother's spirit! If you want to change, go to the mountain where the lights touch the earth. He'll help you make up for what you've done wrong."

Kenai was shocked. "But . . . I didn't do anything wrong," he began. But Tanana had already disappeared.

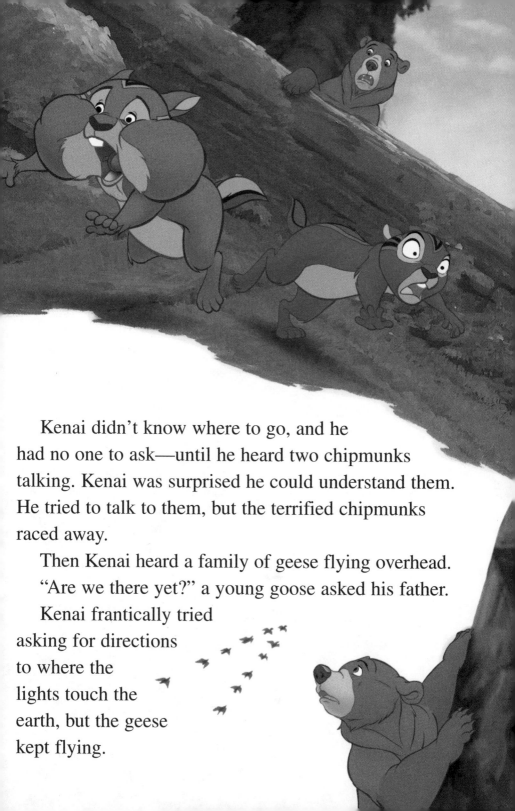

Kenai didn't know where to go, and he
had no one to ask—until he heard two chipmunks
talking. Kenai was surprised he could understand them.
He tried to talk to them, but the terrified chipmunks
raced away.

Then Kenai heard a family of geese flying overhead.
"Are we there yet?" a young goose asked his father.
Kenai frantically tried
asking for directions
to where the
lights touch the
earth, but the geese
kept flying.

Two moose brothers named Rutt and
Tuke were watching Kenai.

"What's he getting all worked up about?"
said the moose named Tuke.

"Maybe the goose pooped on him, eh?"
said Rutt, laughing.

But the moose
stopped laughing when
they saw that the
bear was headed
for them.

"How's it going, bear?" asked Tuke, a little nervously.

"I'm not a bear. I hate bears," answered Kenai.

"Well, gee, you're one big beaver!" said Rutt.

"I'm NOT a beaver! I'm a bear. No, I mean I'm not a bear, I'm a man!" Kenai shouted. "I was transformed into a bear. Magically."

The moose thought Kenai was crazy and decided to play along.

"Oh, yeah, we're not moose either. We're . . . squirrels," Tuke offered.

"Why am I even talking to a couple of dumb moose?" Kenai wondered, as he stomped off.

Almost immediately, Kenai's foot
was caught in a trap. He swung in the
air from one leg, struggling to get free.
    A bear cub named Koda stepped out
of the bushes and offered to help Kenai.
But Kenai didn't want a bear's help—
especially a chatty little cub like Koda.

Kenai tried to free himself, but it was no use. And Koda just wouldn't leave.

"Don't you have somewhere to go?" asked Kenai.

"Yeah, the Salmon Run," answered Koda. "How about this? I get you down. Then we go together?"

Kenai was so exhausted that he agreed to go to the Salmon Run if Koda would free him.

With that, Koda sprang the trap and Kenai crashed to the ground.

Just then Koda sniffed the air. He could smell an approaching hunter! "Run!" he cried, as he scampered off.

The hunter was Denahi! Kenai cried, "Denahi, it's me—Kenai!"

But all Denahi heard was growling. To Denahi, this was the bear that had killed Kenai. He threw his spear, but missed.

Kenai realized Denahi was hunting him and ran away.

Kenai ducked into the same ice cave where Koda
was hiding. Kenai told the little bear that he wasn't
going to go to the Salmon Run.

So Koda told Kenai the truth: A hunter had caused
him and his mother to be separated. Koda's only hope
of finding her was to go to the Salmon Run. Still,
Kenai refused to go.

"C'mon, please? Every night we watch the lights
touch the mountain," pleaded Koda.

"You're kidding me!" said Kenai excitedly. That
was the place where he could be changed back into a
man! Kenai agreed to go with the little cub.

The next morning, the two bears set out.
At first Kenai was annoyed by
Koda's constant chatter and
silly games. But after a
while, Kenai joined in
and even had some fun.

Once again, Rutt and Tuke appeared. "There's a hunter followin' us," Rutt explained. The two moose wanted the bears to protect them.

Kenai knew the hunter was Denahi. And he had a plan to keep Denahi from following their tracks. The group, along with some other animals, found a herd of mammoths and hitched a ride on their backs.

That night, as they watched the lights in the
northern sky, Koda said, "Mom says the spirits make
magical changes in the world."

"My brother Sitka is a spirit," explained Kenai. "If
it wasn't for him, I wouldn't be here." Then Kenai
added, "He was killed by a monster."

Koda looked up at the lights and said, "Thanks,
Sitka. If it weren't for you, I would have never
met Kenai." Then Koda said to Kenai, "I always
wanted a brother." Touched, Kenai let the
cub sleep next to him.

The next morning, the two bears headed off by themselves. They came to a cave covered with paintings. As they looked at one painting of a hunter facing a fierce bear, Koda said, "Those monsters are really scary—especially with those sticks."

Kenai was shocked to learn Koda saw humans as monsters. Kenai had thought the bears were the monsters. But now Kenai wasn't sure what he believed.

Later, the two bears came to a valley with spurting geysers. Koda remembered that the Salmon Run was just on the other side. As they made their way through the valley, the little bear was as playful as ever. But suddenly Koda stopped playing.

THWACK! A spear just missed Kenai by inches! Denahi had found them!

Kenai grabbed Koda and rushed towards a log bridge. They were halfway across the bridge when Denahi cut the log loose. Kenai tossed Koda up to safe ground, then scrambled to safety just as the bridge collapsed.

Denahi screamed in rage as the bears got away. When Kenai looked back, he felt very sad that his brother did not know him.

Before long, Kenai and Koda
reached the Salmon Run. At first
Kenai was scared to be among
the huge bears. But they were
friendly and welcomed him
as part of the family.

Awhile later, Kenai
was learning to fish just
like the other bears.

Although Koda was sad
to learn that his mother
wasn't there yet, he was
happy to be with his
bear pals again.

Soon Kenai and
Koda were having fun.

Later in the day, the bears gathered around to tell stories of what they had done in the past year. Kenai explained that he'd been on the hardest journey of his life with the biggest pain in the neck he had ever met. "But what do you expect from a little brother?" Kenai added, looking at Koda.

Then it was Koda's turn. He told a story of his mother protecting him from some hunters. She and one of the hunters had plunged into the river when the hunter had cracked the ice.

Kenai couldn't believe what he was hearing. Koda was telling the story of the day his brother Sitka was killed by a bear. Now he knew it was also the story of a mother bear protecting her cub.

"She got out of the water okay," continued Koda. "That's how we got separated. Right after that, I met Kenai."

Hearing this, Kenai realized that the bear he had killed was Koda's mother! Kenai felt terrible.

Kenai felt so badly that he ran away. But Koda finally found him. Kenai knew he had to tell the cub the truth.

"Koda," Kenai began, "I have a story to tell you . . . it's mostly about a monster." Then Kenai explained he had done something very wrong. "Your mother's not coming back," he finished sadly.

Overwhelmed by the news, Koda ran away from Kenai.

Having no way to make things better, Kenai began to climb the mountain where the lights touch the earth.

After he reached the top, Kenai called for Sitka. A strange figure moved towards Kenai. It was Denahi! But Denahi did not see his brother Kenai. What he saw was the bear on whom he had sworn revenge. Denahi ran at Kenai with his spear.

Just then Koda came charging
to protect Kenai. The little cub
had decided to follow Kenai after
all. He knocked into Denahi and
ran off with his spear. Denahi
angrily took off after Koda.

"Leave him alone!" roared Kenai,
risking his own life to protect Koda.

Suddenly there was a large flash of light.

A great eagle
appeared and picked
Kenai off the ground.
Magical lights began
to swirl. Kenai was a
human once again.
Denahi was confused
and amazed. The bear
he had just been trying
to kill was his brother!

The eagle spirit of Sitka had turned Kenai into a bear to help him learn his gift of love. As a bear, Kenai had just demonstrated a deep love for Koda. He was willing to give his own life to protect him.

Awestruck, Kenai looked down at his human body as Sitka changed from an eagle to his human spirit form.

Then Kenai spotted a
terrified Koda hiding
behind a boulder.

"Koda, don't be afraid,"
said Kenai. "It's me."

Denahi placed the bear totem around Kenai's neck. The totem reminded Kenai that little Koda needed someone to protect him. "He needs me," Kenai explained to his brothers. He wanted to be a bear again.

"It's all right," said Denahi. "No matter what you choose, you will always be my little brother."

The two brothers embraced.
Then with a burst of swirling
light, Sitka turned Kenai
back into a bear again.

Denahi looked up
at his brother, who
was now an
enormous bear.
"Did I say *little?*"

Then Kenai,
Denahi, and Koda
watched the sky as
Sitka turned into an eagle
and flew back into the magical
lights to join the Great Spirits.

It was time for another ceremony in the village. It was Kenai's turn to put his mark on the ceremonial wall to prove that he had learned the way of his totem and was now an adult.

With Koda and the villagers watching, Denahi helped Kenai place his paw print on the wall among

the handprints of their ancestors.
    The paw print would help
future generations remember
this tale of love and
brotherhood.